THE MANAGER'S POCKET GUIDE TO

 ## ORGANIZATIONAL LEARNING

by Stephen J. Gill

HRD PRESS
Amherst, Massachusetts

Published by:

HRD Press
22 Amherst Road
Amherst, MA 01002
1-800-822-2801
1-413-253-3488
1-413-253-3490 (Fax)
www.hrdpress.com

Printed in Canada

ISBN 0-87425-588-0

Cover design by Eileen Klockars

Production services by CompuDesign

Editorial services by Robie Grant

TABLE OF CONTENTS

Chapter VII

Chapter VIII

Chapter IX

Chapter X

ACKNOWLEDGMENTS

This book has benefited considerably from the advice of three people who have and continue to contribute to my own learning: Nanette Gill, Janet Callaway, and Kathleen Zurcher. I also wish to express my appreciation to Chris Hunter, Vice-President at HRD Press, whose ideas, patience, and encouragement made this work possible.

INTRODUCTION

If you are a manager in an organization that strives for high performance, you face tremendous challenges in today's environment. You don't have to be told this, because you already know. You see these challenges every day: constant change in customers and markets, in ways of doing business, and in technology; workers who are more loyal to their careers than to your organization; a workforce that is diverse in culture, language, and expectations; top management that wants you to keep employees happy while at the same time demanding that you increase productivity.

You ask yourself:

- How can I develop and keep good employees?

- How can I develop leaders, for now and for the future?

- How can I become more effective as a team member, team leader, and supervisor?

- How can I most effectively deal with performance problems?

- How can I help employees learn their new and often changing jobs quickly, so that we do not lose time and money?

- How can I help employees learn what they need to know *without* pulling them away from their jobs?

- How can I help employees get up-to-speed on our new products and services quickly?

- Why don't employees treat customers with more respect and provide them with better service?

- Why don't employees treat each other with more respect, and learn how to cooperate?

- How can I find the time to do my job?

You will not find the answers to these questions in a college classroom or in a management book. Those resources can help you frame the concepts and theory for understanding the questions and offer possible answers to the questions, but taking the best course of action requires that you continually learn. It requires that you learn with an organizational focus and purpose. It requires that you look past the individual to the myriad of factors that affect organizational performance and ask, "What is it about the structure of my organization that is contributing to this behavior, and what can I do about it?"

This kind of learning has been labeled *organizational learning*. Organizational learning is the process of forming and applying collective knowledge to problems and needs. It is the kind of learning that helps the organization continually improve, achieve goals, and attain new possibilities and capacities. It is the kind of learning that taps into employee aspirations, fueling commitment and creating the energy to change.

An organization learns when its employees are continuously creating, organizing, storing, retrieving, interpreting, and applying information. This information becomes knowledge (and, hopefully, wisdom) about improving the work environment, improving performance, improving business processes, and achieving long-range goals that will make the organization successful. The learning is intentional; it is for the benefit of the organization as a whole.

Traditional thinking about learning stops at individual training and skill development. However, today's complexity demands that we think about learning as part of everything we do—individually, in small groups, and as a total organization.

About This Pocket Guide

This guidebook is intended to be a handy, easy-to-use reference for your day-to-day work as a manager. Whether you work in a large or small business, a nonprofit service organization, or a government agency, I want to provide you with some ideas and strategies that will help you enhance learning within your organization.

But I do not want to mislead you. Organizational learning is *not* a simple process and it is *not* about relying on your training department to teach you what you need to know. It is not simply following someone else's recipe either; it is becoming a *chef*. Organizational learning must become embedded in the culture of the organization. Leaders must constantly reexamine these ideas about how to be effective and engage in long-term effort to change the day-to-day behaviors and practices of individuals, groups, and the organization as a whole. This kind of learning requires commitment and leadership.

I have organized the ideas and strategies into three levels: individual learning, small-group learning, and whole-organization learning, but many of the techniques can be applied effectively at more than one level. The categorization simply makes it easier to identify and select strategies that fit problems, challenges, and needs as they arise within your organization.

The strategies outlined in this Pocket Guide have helped private organizations in business and industry, government agencies, and the nonprofit sector. However, nobody can tell you what will work best in your organization. You have to be willing to experiment, try a strategy, evaluate its impact on learning, and make changes if it does not have the impact you want, and try again. Take the time. There are no quick fixes.

This is not an operations manual and it is not meant to be an exhaustive resource. I have tried to provide you with enough information to help you identify potentially useful learning strategies. If something sounds like it might have a useful application in your organization, read more about it in the resources section of the book. If you can, talk to people who have implemented an organizational learning approach in their own organizations. Then, work with a team of employees in your organization who can help you adapt the strategy to your particular circumstances. Try it out in a small way first; then evaluate the results, and make changes before you introduce it to the whole organization.

Part One explains the meaning of organizational learning and why it should be important to you. **Part Two** provides short descriptions of organizational learning strategies organized into three levels: individual; small group and team; and whole organization. **Part Three** suggests some ways to create a culture in the organization that supports continuous learning. **Part Four** presents a list of additional resources about organizational learning and about each of the strategies described in Parts Two and Three.

PART ONE

What is organizational learning?

Today's organizations are in the learning business. Years ago, while evaluating a training program in an automobile plant, I was told by a senior line worker that his generation was hired for their backs, not their brains. Now those same front-line, manufacturing jobs require computer skills, advanced math, team decision-making, total quality management, and continuous improvement. Every worker today has to take a constant supply of new information and apply it to his or her job, whether he or she is operating an assembly line, cutting sheet metal for a construction crew, managing a store, supervising a sales district, providing medical services, directing a social service agency, administering a federal agency, or leading a multinational conglomerate. In fact, this learning has become the fundamental nature of work.

The complexity and rapid change of our work today requires what we refer to as *collective learning*. A work team learns how to solve a problem *together*. A large organization learns how to do strategic planning *together*. They do not simply complete the immediate task; they develop the capacity to perform these tasks successfully in the future.

Learning is critical to the survival of organizations in these rapidly changing times. Peter Noer had this to say in *Breaking Free: A Prescription for Personal and Organizational Change*:

> Organizations of the future will not survive without becoming communities of learning. The learning organization is no academic fad or consultant's buzzword. It is absolutely essential for organizations to learn from their environments, to continually adjust to new and changing data, and, just as is the case with the individual, to learn how to learn from an uncertain and unpredictable future.

Daniel Kim defined individual learning in organizations in *The Link between Individual and Organizational Learning* as ". . . increasing one's capacity to take effective action." This capacity is made up of know-how and know-why. The first is the ability to do something and the second is forming concepts and generalizations that explain one's experience. He defined organizational learning in the same way, saying that it increases an organization's capacity to take effective action.

All learning occurs first within individuals, but the collective know-how and know-why of individuals changes the culture, behavior, and effectiveness of the group or whole organization. To that extent, we can safely say that the group or organization is learning. You and each person on your team might have learned how to prepare and monitor a budget, but figuring out how best to handle a major reduction in revenue requires the synergy of the entire group. It is not the sum of the individual learning, but the creativity and information from the interaction of the team members that results in a successful outcome.

David Garvin explains organizational learning in this way:

> Continuous improvement requires a commitment to learning. How, after all, can an organization improve without first learning something new? Solving a problem, introducing a product, and reengineering a process all require seeing the world in a new light and acting accordingly. In the absence of learning, companies—and individuals—simply repeat old practices. Change remains cosmetic, and improvements are either fortuitous or short-lived.

Garvin argues that organizations learn through five main activities: (1) systematic problem-solving; (2) experimentation with new approaches; (3) learning from their own experience and past history; (4) learning from the experiences and best practices of others; and (5) transferring knowledge quickly and efficiently throughout the organization.

Organizational Learning and Individual Training

Organizational learning does not refer to training events such as classes, workshops, and seminars. We automatically think that attending a workshop, reading professional material, listening to or watching taped presentations, or participating in a computer-based program will produce workplace learning. This notion stems from an old paradigm of instruction that learning must be structured and instructor-directed and be based on new information from an expert. This way of thinking denies all of the various ways in which people actually learn in the workplace. In fact, employees learn most of what they need to know from co-workers, on the job.

Employees do not need to participate in training programs in order to learn. Training events might contribute to individual learning, but they are not sufficient for individual, team, or organizational success because they are not generally linked to the business objectives and strategic goals of the organization. The information conveyed is not necessarily applied in the workplace, and the events rarely involve everyone in the organization who needs the learning. The content is often not central to the work of employees, either. Training is usually done on an occasional basis; learning, however, has to take place continually. It needs to be ongoing and constant.

Organizational learning is the result of an ongoing process that includes the following:

1. Assimilating information.

2. Translating that information into knowledge.

3. Applying that knowledge to real needs.

4. Receiving feedback to revise the information and reshape the knowledge.

Training programs might contribute to organizational learning, but they are not sufficient partly because training occurs at only brief points in time. Learning, when the organization is receptive, is continuous.

If the learning in your organization is to be effective, everyone within it must share and internalize a common set of beliefs. Check your readiness for organizational learning by asking yourself whether you agree or disagree with each of the following principles of organizational learning listed on page 7.

PRINCIPLES OF ORGANIZATIONAL LEARNING

Principles of Organizational Learning	Agree	Disagree
Organizations are systems of people, processes, resources, structures, and culture; a change in any of these elements changes the organization.	_____	_____
All organization activities are elements of processes that can be continuously improved, in part, through knowledge enhancement.	_____	_____
There are no quick fixes to organizational learning deficits.	_____	_____
A long-term view of learning is needed in order to have meaningful results.	_____	_____
You cannot change everything at once; learning must be leveraged so that relatively small interventions result in long-term major changes for the organization.	_____	_____
All employees are responsible for the systems in which they work.	_____	_____

These beliefs must be commonly shared by employees as well as by customers and suppliers. Brinkerhoff and Gill refer to these beliefs as *learning alliances*. Over time, effective learning alliances will result in accumulated knowledge, which is among the most valuable assets of any company—as important as property and inventory, equipment and machines, products and services, and the loyalty of employees and customers.

Levels of Learning

Three levels of learning interact to make up organizational learning: individual learning, small-group learning, and whole-organization learning.

This integration of individual, small-group, and whole-organization learning can be likened to the learning that takes place within a flock of geese: in the spring, each newborn chick learns quickly how to survive through a combination of instinct, imprinting, modeling, and reinforcement. Soon the brood of chicks is walking in single file behind their mother under the protective gaze of their father. This family group is constantly together, searching for food and interacting with their surroundings. By late spring, each family of fully grown geese has joined other families, flying together in perfect formation, sharing leadership, and cooperating as a community for the safety and benefit of all. The results of individual, small-group, and whole-organization learning can be seen within the span of a few short months.

I. Individual Learning

Individual learning occurs as each employee acquires the knowledge, develops the skills, and adopts the attitudes and beliefs

Levels of Learning Complexity

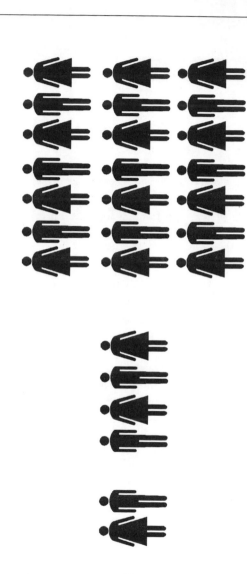

Individual Learning   Small-Group Learning   Whole-Organization Learning

that will help the organization succeed (however success is defined). It prepares employees for the inevitable changes that will occur in the goals and work processes of the organization, and creates greater self-awareness. Peter Senge calls this the discipline of personal mastery. Daniel Goleman believes that this is how we develop *emotional intelligence*: the self-awareness and sense of competence that allows one to take risks, accept feedback, learn from successes and mistakes, relate effectively to others, and stay focused on personal goals

2. Small-Group Learning

Small-group learning occurs as the members of a group discover together how best to contribute to the performance of the group as a whole. They learn from and about each other, they learn how to work effectively as a group, and they learn how to apply that knowledge in order to achieve the purposes of the group. Not all groups in the workplace are teams Katzenbach and Smith contend, but all groups can achieve some group learning. Teams share goals and place a value on member interaction; this is why they achieve more "group learning" than other types of groups in the workplace.

Team learning has been referred to as ". . . a continuous process by which team members acquire knowledge about the larger organization, the team, and the individual team members" (Russ-Eft et al). This knowledge resides with the team as a whole, but not with any single individual, and it is why the team is so effective: it works toward shared goals and shared processes for achieving those goals.

3. Whole-Organization Learning

Whole-organization learning refers to the ". . . ongoing processes and integrated systems that facilitate individuals' and teams' ability to learn, grow, and change as a result of organizational experiences" (Russ-Eft et al). This occurs when managers eliminate boundaries that prevent the free flow of information across the organization—something Ashkenas and others refer to as "the boundary-less organization." Managers should ask themselves: What can I do to help this organization learn about itself? What can I do to help this organization learn what will result in new knowledge, skills, attitudes, and beliefs? What can I do to help this organization learn how to create a culture of learning? How can I be a "merchant of light" that illuminates a challenge so that others can see?

Whole-organization learning is achieving a shared understanding throughout the organization, and then creating the capacity throughout the organization to improve processes and achieve strategic goals. As Marquardt explains it in *Building the Learning Organization*:

> . . . organizational learning occurs through the shared insights, knowledge, and mental models of members of the organization . . . organizational learning builds on past knowledge and experience—that is, on organizational memory, which depends on institutional mechanisms (e.g., policies, strategies, and explicit models) used to retain knowledge.

CHAPTER III

Learning How to Learn

What have you tried to learn recently? A musical instrument? A new computer program? A dance step? Cross-country skiing, or inline skating?

And how did you approach the task of learning?

- Did you read about it first, or discuss it with experts?

- Did you watch or listen to others doing it?

- Did you carefully analyze their behavior, or did you fix a mental image of the skill in your mind?

- Did you hire a coach or attend a class?

- Or, did you just start doing it, learning from trial and error?

Each of these strategies represents different ways in which individuals prefer to learn a new skill. There is no one right way— just different ways that have preference, depending on individual life experiences, the way people process information in their brains, the specific circumstances of the learning, or the attitudes toward the skill. You can maximize learning by being aware of how your employees prefer to learn in a given situation and helping them to use a variety of strategies to facilitate their learning. In short, helping them *learn how to learn*.

Start by noticing how *you* learn best in different situations—the conditions, and why you learn best under those conditions. This means taking a mental step back from the learning process and analyzing what it is about the process that helps you learn and what the barriers are that prevent you from learning. Perhaps the best way for you to learn how to use new accounting software, for example, is by trial and error: you like to figure things out as you go along. In another situation such as giving performance feedback to someone you supervise, for example, you might prefer to role play the situation and have an experienced coach observe your interaction with the employee and evaluate your actions. Another manager might prefer to read about these skills first, or talk about them with colleagues, or see a video model of the skills that are needed. These are different methods of learning that need to be matched with the learner.

When you understand your own learning style, you can help others learn how to learn

- about themselves
- about how to interact effectively with others
- about the technical skills needed to do their jobs
- about the organization's vision, mission, values, guiding principles, and strategic goals
- about their customers, clients, and stakeholders
- about business processes

- about the external environment
- about the future and how it will affect their activities

You can help yourself and show others how their individual behavior can unintentionally contribute to the organization's problems. For example, senior managers who deny their own obvious responsibility for problems send a message to others that the organization does not value individual learning and improvement.

Small groups are often ineffective because they do not address internal dynamics or process issues; they are likely to repeat their failures and not improve on their weaknesses, thus they are not able to take full advantage of their strengths. This goes for the process of interacting and making decisions, as well as performing the actual task: some boards of directors of companies will meet monthly for years, going through the same agenda each time, never discussing strategic direction or leadership. Meanwhile, the company goes into deep debt, loses market share, and becomes unprofitable. Boards of directors may possess great power or status, but they face the same problems of any small group if they do not learn how to learn together.

"We keep reinventing the wheel."

"The left hand does not know what the right hand is doing."

"They are just rearranging the deck chairs on the Titanic."

Sound familiar? These are metaphors for an organization that is not learning to reach its potential. The organization, as a whole, needs to learn how to learn. Organizations must value and support generative learning. They do this by creating mechanisms and procedures for individuals and groups to share their knowledge with each other, and documenting and recording the experiences of people across the organization so that everyone's knowledge and skills are accessible to the entire organization. Everyone in the organization must understand its purpose and develop a shared meaning of their work together—and reflect honestly together on what they have done and how effectively they have done it.

Barriers to Learning

As you try to facilitate organizational learning, you will encounter barriers embedded within the structure of all complex organizations. Argyris labels these barriers resistance to change; unwillingness to discuss the undiscussible; need for control; a short-term focus; simple solutions to complex problems; and the "skilled incompetence" of managers.

1. Resistance to change is the tendency we have to maintain the familiar and avoid trying something new and different. Moving from a command-and-control style of leadership to an empowerment form of leadership, changing over from an elaborate hierarchical organizational structure to a flat, boundaryless organizational structure or even changing individual-centered work processes to team-centered work processes—these are all difficult because employees tend to focus on what problems this will create for them personally, rather than what they will learn from the change process that will build on their strengths and strengthen the organization.

2. Not discussing the undiscussible prevents useful information from surfacing. All work groups and whole organizations agree not to discuss some things; usually, this agreement is implicit—a shared but unspoken understanding that the issue

Barriers to Learning

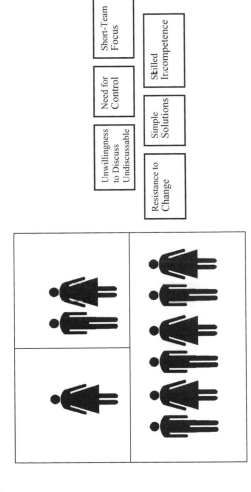

Individuals, Small Groups, and Organizations

Barriers

- Unwillingness to Discuss Undiscussable
- Need for Control
- Short-Team Focus
- Resistance to Change
- Simple Solutions
- Skilled Incompetence

Learning

will not be mentioned. Your subordinates will not talk to you about their dissatisfaction with how much time you spend in the office; your work group will not discuss problems with the CEO's business strategy, which they have been working on for months but think is a waste of time and resources; your co-workers will not confront one another with communication problems for fear of embarrassing someone and then having criticism come back at them. The people who have the information and the person who needs to hear the information are unknowingly colluding with each other: they are preventing discussion of the very things that get in the way of organizational learning.

3. People have a *need for control.* This is manifested in the structures that we build for our organizations: organization charts, policy manuals, published rules and regulations, performance evaluation processes, budget and expenses monitoring, internal security systems, and the design of physical spaces. All these things are ways of exercising control over the behavior of employees, though each is an aspect of organizational culture that holds some value in a large, complex business. They cease adding value when we stop learning from them and about them, however. Continually ask yourself these questions:

- How is this process adding to my understanding of our organization and our business?

- How can this process be improved so that it helps us be more successful in achieving our goals?

4. Short-term, simple solutions to complex problems might provide us with some relief in difficult situations, but do not help us learn. Removing a challenging employee from a team without confronting the problem that the employee is surfacing or deciding that you will review all expenses submitted for reimbursement because you suspect that people are padding reimbursement requests, or even using layoffs to reduce costs before first examining the entire enterprise for other opportunities to control costs or increase revenue are all examples of actions that might be necessary but usually represent short-term, simple solutions. These kinds of situations offer tremendous opportunities for learning for everyone in the organization. If you take the easy way out and fail to invest time, effort, resources, and emotion in the big picture and long view you may find temporary relief, but nobody will learn; the problems will continue because nothing will have changed in the elements of the organization's structure that are producing these problems.

5. *Skilled incompetence* is a strong, but accurate description of a common operative disease: our natural tendency as managers to avoid embarrassing or threatening interactions with others by changing the subject, placing blame on others, or not accepting responsibility for problem situations. When we do this, we miss out on an opportunity to learn from others and reflect on our own behavior. To learn, you must ask yourself, What is it about what I am doing or saying that contributes to other people behaving in ineffective and destructive ways? You will need feedback from others to answer this question, and you will have to listen non-defensively to the answers. Learn from the experience of those managers who have already gone down this path and learned from their mistakes.

As a manager, you can strengthen your organization by helping individuals, teams, and the organization as a whole get past the barriers and open themselves up to the possibility of learning and change. Start by using the worksheet that follows to assess where your organization stands in terms of these barriers.

BARRIERS TO LEARNING: WORKSHEET

What have you observed in your organization that indicates . . .

Resistance to change?

Not discussing the undiscussable?

Need for control?

Focusing on short-term, simple solutions?

Skilled incompetence?

Principles of Individual Learning

Much has been studied and written about how adults learn. For our purpose here, we will focus on what researchers identify as key principles that describe most adults most of the time (there are exceptions). Keep these twelve principles in mind as you design learning experiences for yourself and for your employees, and as you help employees design their own learning experiences.

12 PRINCIPLES OF ADULT LEARNING

1. No two people learn in exactly the same way.

2. Employees can be ordered to do something new, but they cannot be forced to learn.

3. Adults are motivated to learn by significant work and life changes, and when they believe that what they will learn will help them cope with those changes.

4. For some employees, learning is its own reward; for most employees, learning is a means to an end.

5. Enhanced self-esteem and pleasure are strong secondary motivators of learning.

6. Adults have teachable moments, when the timing of learning is critical to its success and retention.

7. Employees want the opportunity to apply newly learned knowledge and skills to relevant problems in the organization.

8. Adults learn best when they can integrate new information with what they already know.

9. Fast-paced, complex, and unusual learning tasks interfere with learning for adults.

10. Adults tend to let their own errors affect their self-esteem, which causes them to avoid risk by resorting to old ways of doing things.

11. Adults prefer to have a say about the design and direction of their learning experiences.

12. Adults prefer learning experiences that provide opportunities for interaction with their peers.

Ground Rules for Small-group Learning

Simply being together in a group does not guarantee that the group will learn from its work. You must create an environment in which groups can learn and individuals can learn in groups. Use the following ground rules for small-group learning to create the environment.

12 GROUND RULES FOR SMALL-GROUP LEARNING

1. Respect individual differences, and express appreciation for and use the knowledge and skills of each individual in the group.

2. Listen to (don't just hear) what group members say to you and to each other; try to listen to the other person without listening to yourself.

3. Attend to the quality of group process (how people work together), as well as to the effectiveness of the group in completing the task (assignment).

4. Invite ideas, suggestions, and reactions from all of the group members.

5. Look for and make explicit the connections among ideas that are expressed by everyone.

6. Encourage members to try out the ideas of others without ridicule, embarrassment, or punishment from the members who contribute the ideas.

7. Surface problems and conflicts among members and work at resolving these as a group.

12 GROUND RULES FOR SMALL-GROUP LEARNING (continued)

8. Document what the group has learned, and reinforce this learning over time. Include multiple sources of information to verify learning; separate hunches from evidence.

9. Play down the organizational status differences among individuals when working in the group.

10. Assess the group's learning needs, both process and task, and provide learning opportunities; employ multiple learning strategies that fit the diverse styles within the group.

11. Apply the "both/and" principle: When two ideas seem contradictory on the surface, suggest that the lesson might be that "both _____ and _____ " might be true. Resist either/or dichotomies.

12. Ask "learning questions" in order to focus participants on particular strategic lessons. Prioritize potential group learning questions by asking, "How would this area of learning influence the effectiveness or efficiency of our work if we pursued it? Would anyone use the learning? How?"

Conditions for Organizational Learning

Organizational learning occurs in many different ways, but is most effective when eight basic conditions are met. Use the following worksheet to assess your organization.

WORKSHEET: CONDITIONS FOR ORGANIZATIONAL LEARNING

How typical are the following conditions in your organization. Are they very, somewhat, or not at all typical?

	Very	Somewhat	Not at all
1. Senior management is committed to learning; they demonstrate this commitment through their own behavior.	____	____	____
2. Everyone believes that learning is their personal responsibility.	____	____	____
3. Learning is encouraged at three levels: individual, small-group, and whole-organization.	____	____	____
4. Risk is encouraged and not punished; failures are learning opportunities.	____	____	____
5. Learning is linked to the organization's goals.	____	____	____
6. Information is stored in such a way that it can be retrieved when and where it is needed.	____	____	____

WORKSHEET: CONDITIONS FOR ORGANIZATIONAL LEARNING (continued)

How typical are the following conditions in your organization. Are they very, somewhat, or not at all typical?

	Very	Somewhat	Not at all
7. **Learning and the process of learning is measured; these findings are used to enhance learning within the organization.**	____	____	____
8. **People are given feedback; the results of performance are communicated to participants in the organization in order to develop new insights and influence their behavior.**	____	____	____

Reflection and Feedback

Reflection and feedback are the core competencies of organizational learning. **Reflection** is looking at ourselves honestly, without excuses, and analyzing the strengths and weaknesses of what we say and do. Reflection also offers us the opportunity to learn from experience: You cannot learn from experience unless you consciously take the time and make the effort to stand back and look at your behavior in the organization, as if holding up a mirror and saying to yourself, What do I like in the image? What do I want to change? Individuals, groups, and organizations as a whole can hold up the mirror and ask these questions of themselves.

Feedback, in the organizational learning sense of this term, is the ability to analyze a situation and tell others how what they have said or done has affected us, and then be open to their reactions. Feedback helps people learn from their own behavior; it adds to what each person might be learning from reflection. Feedback mechanisms can be built into the organization so that individuals, groups, and the organization as a whole are continuously receiving information that they can use for improvement.

The chart that follows provides some helpful guidelines for using feedback.

GUIDELINES FOR USING FEEDBACK

1. Look at feedback as a gift—be open and receptive to it, and even encourage it. Ask for feedback from all your customers, your employees, your direct reports and peers, and anyone else who can help you learn and grow as a person, as a professional, and as a leader of your organization.

2. Work on developing self-mastery—the interpersonal style needed to genuinely encourage others to provide feedback, and the mental attitude needed to stay receptive, even when feedback is negative. Don't be defensive, and always thank the feedback-giver. Remember: You're the one who decides, after some reflection, whether the feedback merits action, and if so, what action.

GUIDELINES FOR USING FEEDBACK (continued)

3. Make sure that feedback in your organization is received and applied in the context of the entire system. Limiting feedback to select levels is like limiting team-performance results to select team members: It makes no sense at all, especially if changes are needed. And don't forget, customer feedback is the real gift you need to actively seek out, over and over again.

4. Bring to your organization all that you personally learn about feedback, receptivity, flexibility, and adaptability. The more senior your level in the organization, the more important this is.

(Adapted from *The Manager's Pocket Guide to Systems Thinking and Learning,* by Stephen G. Haines. Amherst: HRD Press, 1998, p. 47.)

CHAPTER IV

Managers as Model Learners

As a manager, your role must be to model organizational learning behavior. If you want others to be constantly learning, you must set an example for them. If you say that you want teams to reflect on their actions, derive lessons from their experiences, and share these lessons with others, then you must do this yourself, and make this visible to the group.

> To create a community of learners, leaders must be learners themselves.

In the current environment of major structural changes, a leader must be at the vanguard of organizational change, questioning long-held corporate beliefs and assumptions, asking new questions, not just seeking new answers. Becoming a catalyst of paradigm shifts means more than acquiring new skills: it requires assuming a whole new way of being—as a theory-builder, a visionary, and a learner. In the new model, leaders will build and nurture learning organizations. They will be responsible for enhancing the quality of their thinking, not just the quality of their doing. This means becoming theory-builders: creating new frameworks for continually testing strategies, policies, and decisions . . . leaders must have the courage to become learners themselves . . . Becoming a true learner may be the most difficult shift that a leader makes. (Daniel H. Kim, 1993)

Chris Argyris said this about learning in *Teaching Smart People How to Learn*: "Success in the market-place increasingly depends on learning, yet most people don't know how to learn. What's more, those members of the organization that many assume to be the best at learning are, in fact, not very good at it." He is referring to highly educated professionals who hold key leadership positions. Often, they learn just enough to make incremental improvement in a process. Managers as well as employees, he writes, must ". . . reflect critically on their own behavior, identify the ways they often inadvertently contribute to the organization's problems, and then change how they act."

Argyris argues that managers need to think differently if they want to break down defensive reasoning. They have to learn how to learn from failure. Even though our natural tendency is to reject criticism, and to find other people and situations to blame for the problem, we have to learn new ways of looking and thinking about our own behavior.

People want to perform effectively and be thought of as competent. Your example will motivate others to learn new ways to reason through a problem. "People can learn to recognize the reasoning behind their actions. They can face up to the fact that they unconsciously design and implement actions that they do not intend. Finally, people can learn how to identify what individuals and groups do to create patterns of

30

organizational defenses and how these defenses contribute to an organization's problems.

Change in defensive reasoning has to start at the top. Senior management must be honest about problem situations, examine the data about these situations, challenge the inferences that are made about this data, and then make decisions that fit the new awareness.

PART TWO

What are the strategies that result in organizational learning?

This section organizes a variety of organizational learning strategies into individual, small-group, and whole-organization categories in order to provide a starting point to facilitate learning. However, we seldom learn in one isolated way: the most productive learning occurs when all three levels are operating simultaneously and synergistically.

CHAPTER V

Individual Learning

The one way we know we can learn continually is by paying constant attention to our environment and the people and information around us. If you touch a hot stove, you learn to not do that again. If you read about fitness in a magazine, you might learn a strengthening exercise that will help your back muscles. If a friend gives you advice on how to handle a problem in your family, you might learn a way to interact effectively with relatives. All of these are examples of important individual learning. Organizational learning, however, is different.

Organizational learning at the individual level is about:

- Discovering how you work and learn best.

- Achieving greater awareness of your own values and goals.

- Achieving greater awareness of what you do well and what you need to improve.

- Balancing work, family, and leisure activities.

- Knowing how you fit into the direction of the organization.

- Knowing what you have to do to help the organization succeed.

- Creating new approaches to old problems.

Organizational learning by individuals is learning that is linked to the goals of the organization: an employee who becomes a more effective member of the organization, but also an employee who is learning with the intent of building his/her individual capacity to help the organization achieve its potential.

This kind of learning requires alignment. That is, what is being learned must be consistent with the desired results for the organization. You are learning project-management skills because you are taking on the leadership role in a major project that will help the company expand its market share in a target population, which the company needs in order to continue to grow. You are not learning project-management skills just because the course is available, or because you have money in your budget, or because everyone else is doing it.

People do not learn from formal training events unless they are prepared and motivated to learn before the event, and unless their learning is reinforced, applied, and given feedback during and after the event. This might be an over-simplification of the process, but try to think of learning as having a *before*, *during*, and *after* phase in relation to the content to be learned. For example, let's say that your company needs to be better at managing projects. Simply sending employees to a project-management workshop where they are taught how to plan a project and use software to manage the project is not sufficient. They must be prepared to learn about project management before the training event, and they must be helped to apply what they were taught about project management after the training event. Otherwise, the employees will not apply the information and the training will be a waste of resources.

Use the following checklist as a guide for attending to the *before*, the *during,* and the *after* of training events.

CHECKLIST FOR INDIVIDUAL LEARNING

Before holding a learning event, help individual employees:

- ☐ Understand how their performance must change to help the organization meet its goals.
- ☐ Understand the goals and objectives of the event.
- ☐ Have reasonable expectations for their own performance during and after the learning event.
- ☐ Arrange an opportunity to apply the new knowledge, skills, beliefs, and attitudes immediately after the event.
- ☐ Feel the support and encouragement that you have for their learning and performance improvement.

During the learning event, help individual employees:

- ☐ Understand what they will have to do to apply the new knowledge, skills, beliefs, and attitudes to their work.
- ☐ Explain what they are learning to others.
- ☐ Practice the skills from the event.
- ☐ Receive feedback on their knowledge and skills.
- ☐ Be prepared for any obstacles in the workplace that might interfere with their performance of the new skills.
- ☐ Feel the support and encouragement that you have for their learning and performance improvement.

Adapted from *The Learning Alliance*, Robert Brukerhoff and S.J. Gill. Jossey-Bass, 1994.

CHECKLIST FOR INDIVIDUAL LEARNING (continued)

After the event, help individual employees:

- ❑ Apply the new knowledge, skills, beliefs, and attitudes to their work.
- ❑ Receive rewards for learning and application to their work.
- ❑ Remove any obstacles to applying the learning.
- ❑ Receive feedback on how well they are performing.
- ❑ Understand additional learning needs and how to meet these needs.
- ❑ Understand how their continuous learning will help the organization achieve its goals.
- ❑ Feel the support and encouragement that you have for their learning and performance improvement

Think of an employee or a team and what they need to learn in order to enhance their capacity. Then think of a learning event that might facilitate this learning, such as a workshop, seminar, computer-based course, videotape, audiotape, or reading material. Fill out the Learning Process Chart. What are you willing to do or help do before, during, and after the learning event to ensure that learning occurs and that the new knowledge, skills, beliefs, and attitudes are applied over time?

If your company has a training department, it can be a useful resource in helping employees learn. As a manager, however, you are a much more important part of the learning process for the employees you supervise. Your support for an employee's learning before, during, and after the formal intake of information is critical to organizational learning. Learning will be optimized if you form a learning alliance with the learner.

Learning Process Chart

Instructors: Think of an employee or team and their learning needs. Fill in this chart with what you will help them to do before, during, and after the learning event. What are the restraining and driving forces for learning in your organization?

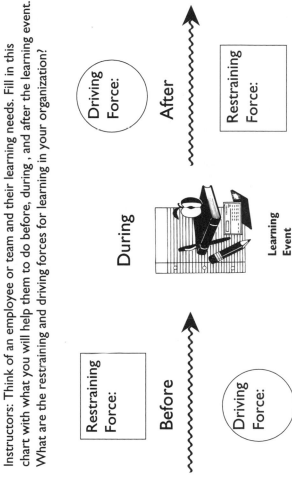

Before

Restraining Force:

Driving Force:

During

Learning Event

After

Driving Force:

Restraining Force:

These steps will help you form and maintain such an alliance:

THE LEARNING ALLIANCE

1. Discuss what the employee needs to learn in order to help your business unit achieve its objectives and the organization's strategic goals.

2. Agree on a set of learning objectives with the employee.

3. Decide together what will indicate that the learning was achieved.

4. Review the strategies for learning, and decide together which strategies might be most effective in helping this employee learn.

5. Help the employee arrange to use the appropriate resources in a just-in-time manner.

6. Plan frequent, regular, and brief meetings to discuss progress toward goals and any needed modifications in the process.

7. Change the learning process as needs arise.

CHAPTER VI

Strategies for Individual Learning

Learning at the individual level can be enhanced by the use of specific strategies (a selection of these strategies follows). To have maximum effect, each of these strategies must be tailored to the needs of learners. Learners should work with their supervisors and come to agreement on goals and performance outcomes for the activity. This important question should be answered at the outset: What should the learner get out of this experience, and how should this learning be applied on the job? Having this kind of plan is critical to achieving organizational learning.

Personal Visioning

We are driven by goals. Having a clear image in our minds of what we are trying to become motivates and keeps us focused on what we need to do. A personal vision is a long-term goal that guides our learning. We might not reach that goal, but that is not as important as having a self-development north star to follow. Develop a personal vision for yourself, and help employees develop their own personal learning visions aligned with the vision of your organization.

Individualized Learning Plans

Help your employees develop their own individualized learning plans. These plans are very specific commitments to learning and performance—statements about what knowledge, skills, beliefs, or attitudes the employee intends to acquire, how and when this learning will be applied on the job to achieve organizational goals, and how the organization will know that the performance improvement has occurred. The learning plan can take one of many forms, because it is tailored to the different learning styles and work contexts of each employee.

Gilley, Boughton, and Maycunich describe the process in this way:

> The learning acquisition and transfer process consists of five steps that are mutually completed by managers and employees. They are:
>
> 1. identifying performance objectives
>
> 2. identifying learning resources and strategies
>
> 3. creating transfer-of-learning strategies
>
> 4. identifying target dates for completion of each performance objective
>
> 5. measuring performance enhancement and improvement

Self-Reflection

Set aside time for your own reflection. Select a recent work experience from which you want to learn, such as leading a team meeting, making a presentation to a group, discussing a performance review, or participating in a small-group work session. Ask yourself these questions, developed by Daudelin and Hall:

1. Have any new ideas for me come out of the experience?

2. What ideas stand out as being important to me?

3. How do these ideas relate to other ideas I know about?

4. How can I use these ideas in my work?

5. How did I react to the discussion in these activities?

6. How did I relate (positively and negatively) to other people in the activity? What might have caused me to relate in that way?

7. At what point during the activity did I feel my interest rising? Declining? What might have caused these shifts in my interest?

8. What was it about the experience that made it easy for me to learn? What made it difficult? What does that say about how I prefer to learn?

9. What do I plan to do as a result of what I have learned from this experience?

Logs, Diaries, and Journals

It is important that you record your reflections and learning, perhaps in a log, diary, or journal. If you follow the self-reflection exercise described in the previous section for three or more experiences, you will find yourself becoming more insightful about what you are learning during the actual experience. Recording your observations will become second nature to you and you will find yourself thinking about journal writing following your day-to-day experiences.

Instructor-led Classroom Seminars and Workshops

Business surveys estimate that 80 to 90 percent of all training is delivered through instructor-led seminars and workshops, but many of these experiences are not as effective as we expect them to be. Individual learning can, indeed, take place in seminars and workshops, if the following criteria are met:

- The instructor has expert knowledge that the learners need to know.

- The individual learners will benefit in some way from learning in a group environment.

- The learners will have an opportunity immediately afterwards to apply the new knowledge, skills, beliefs, or attitudes to their work.

The decision to use this teaching format is often made on the basis of tradition (we have always done it this way), efficiency (we can get everyone through in a short time), or expediency (we already have the materials and instructors for the program). These might be good administrative reasons to use a classroom format, but they are not good *learning* reasons. Much of what is taught in this way (an estimated 80 to 90 percent) is not retained by the learner.

If the conditions warrant an instructor-led classroom learning experience, planning will be essential. Classroom instruction (and all of the other learning strategies) has to be designed carefully—so carefully, in fact, that an entire discipline of study has been created around instructional system design.

If you select this learning strategy, be sure you involve professionals who are experienced is this area, as well as content experts. They must collaborate on identifying learning needs, on setting and developing the context for learning and appropriate learning objectives, and creating a curriculum that addresses the breadth of learning that is needed. They must also create classroom experiences that convey the knowledge, skills, beliefs, and attitudes necessary for success, and provide learners with adequate feedback to help them improve.

To maximize learning, the instruction must be designed to achieve specific learning objectives. These objectives provide direction, motivate learners, and shape the content and methods of instruction; they become the criteria for assessing the effectiveness of the instruction.

Therefore, the first step in instructional design is to determine the learning objectives. Involve yourself in the process of finding answers to these key questions:

- What specific knowledge, skills, attitudes, and beliefs do employees need to learn that will help the organization achieve its goals?

- What is the best way to achieve these objectives in a classroom environment?

- How will you know that this learning has occurred?

Creating an effective instructional program to build job skills or help people work more effectively with one another is a four-phase process:

Phase One: Formulate learning goals. Decide what knowledge, skills, attitudes, and beliefs are needed by employees to help the organization become successful.

Phase Two: Plan learning strategies. Decide which learning methods will result in the outcomes necessary for achieving the organization's goals.

Phase Three: Implement learning methods. Keep the focus on the learning outcomes. Adjust methods to make sure that you achieve the desired outcomes.

Phase Four: Support performance improvement. Reinforce that application of learning in the workplace. Provide refresher learning events, job aids, and feedback, as needed.

Job Rotation

Consider switching people around within the organization to provide workers with an opportunity to learn about work processes from different perspectives. This is especially helpful if the jobs are in departments that are suppliers and customers of each other. For example, workers who spend some time in the sales department, some time in the parts department, and some time in the service department of an automobile dealership are better able to understand how these departments can work together to meet the needs of the external customers and achieve the financial goals of the dealership.

However, to achieve learning, everyone must be clear about goals: what they are supposed to learn from each job in the job rotation. Each individualized learning plan should include objectives and how to know when these objectives have been achieved. Time must be set aside for reflection and for feedback from the supervisor, co-workers, and subordinates. Job rotation might appear to be radical at first, but it is an eye-opening experience that can only *help* the organization.

Individual Coaching

Coaching refers to the process of facilitating the self-awareness, learning, and performance improvement of an employee, often on the job. Individual coaching is a learning relationship between two employees: a manager and someone he or she supervises, two managers, or a worker and a co-worker. It is focused on a specific learning need, a performance deficit, or a problem between employees.

Coaching is more than a strategy: it involves listening, asking, and speaking to draw out and augment characteristics and potential that are already present in a person. It is based on the premise that learning will take place in a safe and challenging environment created by someone who will listen without judgment. Listening is the basis for an effective coaching relationship that facilitates learning. The following suggestions for listening effectively have been adapted from *The Fifth Discipline Fieldbook*:

Some Tips for Effective Listening:

- Stop talking to others and to yourself. You can't listen if you are talking. If you are talking to yourself, you are really trying to create an argument in your mind for a particular position you want to take with the person you are coaching.

- Put yourself in the employee's shoes. Imagine yourself in her position, doing her work, facing her problems, using her language, and having her values. (What must she be feeling about the situation?)

- Be interested. Show your interest through your body language and your verbal responses.

47

- Observe body language and other actions to understand the meaning behind the words.

- Don't interrupt unless a short interruption can be used to clarify what the employee is saying to you.

- "Listen between the lines" for what is not being said but what is meant.

- Speak only affirmatively while listening, using only short comments. Resist the temptation to jump in with an evaluative remark. For example, "That's a good thing to do; that is against policy; or I don't agree."

- Rephrase what the other person has just told you at key points in the conversation, such as when the employee has finished speaking about one major idea or experience.

- Again, stop talking to others and to yourself. This is repeated because it is so important.

As a coach, you are creating a partnership that puts the focus on the employee's learning, rather than on your teaching. Your job is to support the learning and performance of another employee. You do this by asking questions and giving feedback in a nonthreatening and nonjudgmental way, so that there are no defensive thoughts and feelings that get in the way of learning. The way to do this is to follow these four steps, adapted from Cory and Bradley:

Step One:
   Ask the person what worked well for him/her during the activity (the meeting, the conversation, the pre-

sentation, the sales call, etc.) and why he/she thinks it worked well.

Step Two:
Ask what didn't work well and why.

Step Three:
Ask what he/she might consider doing differently next time.

Step Four:
Offer any feedback you might have from your perspective. Start with what worked, and then describe the behaviors you observed that didn't work and options for change.

Your job as coach is to reduce or eliminate obstacles to learning. Some of the key obstacles include employee perceptions about one's capability and how that capability appears to others. Here are some examples:

- Wanting to appear competent and knowledgeable

- Assuming that the need to learn indicates a deficiency

- Fear of being judged

- Self-doubt about being able to perform to the expectations of co-workers

- Trying too hard to learn

Coaching is a relationship between a "client" and a coach in which both are learning. The coach focuses on how to facilitate employee learning, rather than on telling employees what they are doing right and wrong (this is what most supervisors do).

You might have a coaching discussion with an employee while he/she is practicing or actually trying to apply new knowledge or skills, but more often, the coaching occurs on-the-fly, and not while employees are applying what they have learned. A delay occurs between the coaching session and application of learning.

Follow-up is essential to ensure learning. Be sure to reinforce the new, positive behavior by praising the employee immediately when you see the desired action ("Good job!"). Your supervisee is more likely to continue this more positive behavior when he or she feels recognized and appreciated for the change.

Mentoring

Mentoring is an active relationship between a mentor (someone with greater experience and expertise) and a mentee for the purpose of personal and professional development. Less structured than management coaching, the mentoring relationship is a learning partnership of mutual respect in which the employee learns from the expertise and experience of the senior person. The mentor must be able to counsel, guide, and teach in a way that is helpful to the employee. Although the mentee is the identified learner in this relationship, both will learn when the mentoring is done well.

Mentors can provide immediate and tailored learning opportunities for the employee—especially helpful for new employees at all levels in an organization who are trying to figure out how they can contribute, relate effectively to their co-workers and supervisors, and gain the respect of others in their new role. Most new employees need a relationship with someone who can provide this guidance.

If you want to be an effective mentor, you must learn to listen —not hear, *listen*. By this I mean that we must put aside our tendency to judge others or persuade or advocate for a particular belief or position. Any of these tactics will simply result in a psychological barrier between you and the person you are trying to help; try to understand employees from *their* point of view.

In most instances, it is not a good idea to act as mentor to any of your direct reports. Your supervisory relationship with them does not usually create the conditions for a good mentoring relationship, and it may cause discord with others.

Once you understand a mentee's problems or needs, try to share any useful information or related experiences you have had that might help the mentee learn from his/her own situations. Learning the ropes in the new company might have been hard for you, but you figured out how to do it. Perhaps you learned what works and what does not work when you needed to put together a core team for a new project; your mentee can learn from your experience. The situation will undoubtedly be different, but together you can decide how to apply the lessons to his/her experience.

Unlike most coaching, mentoring is more of an art than a science. A step-by-step structure does not usually fit: It is the quality of the relationship that determines effectiveness.

Computer Technology

Many of the learning needs of employees can be met through the use of new technology—not to deliver instructor-centered training faster and cheaper, but rather to facilitate just-in-time learning and put the employee in control of an individualized learning process that can be maintained and continually enhanced over time.

Work with staff members from information technology, systems, process design, and training to develop an integrated electronic performance-support system. This is a system of online tools that helps employees learn, when and where they need to in order to enhance their performance on the job.

Here are some options:

- Conferencing:
  This can be used to link people in different locations at the same time for a single event

- Computer-based training (CBT):
  Personal computers can be used for synchronous (at the same time as the instructor) or asynchronous (at the convenience of the learner) instruction; the Internet or an organization's intranet can be used for delivery

- Network information:
  Information needed to build the capacity of the learner can be provided online, via the organization's computer network or intranet

- Computer-supported collaborative work:
  Networked computers equipped with common operating systems and software can be used for collaborative work among teams of learners

The possibilities are expanding every day. Team members separated by thousands of miles can participate in virtual meetings and work on projects together. An employee who forgets how to fill out the company's new purchase-order form can hit a key on her computer, and an online tool will appear on the screen to guide her through the task. After returning from a week-long leadership development workshop, participants can access a window of reinforcing information from the workshop that appears on their computer screens when they log on each day.

On-The-Job Training

A study for the American Society for Training and Development and the U.S. Department of Labor estimated that 80 to 90 percent of an employee's job knowledge and skills comes from on-the-job training (OJT). Think about it: After an initial orientation program (if there is one), where do employees on a manufacturing line or in offices learn how to perform the day-to-day activities of their jobs? Usually at their place of work, from their co-workers, through direct instruction or observation. This is a prime opportunity to facilitate employee learning; ignore it and you will be leaving to serendipity the development of knowledge, skills, attitudes, and beliefs that your employees need to help the organization reach its potential.

Structured OJT:
The planned process of developing task-level expertise by having an experienced employee train a novice employee at or near the actual work setting. (Jacobs, 1995)

All employees must perform certain job tasks, such as solving problems, making decisions, inspecting products and processes, following procedures, planning and organizing resources, and using tools. You can help an employee learn to perform these tasks by planning and executing OJT. The process will vary depending on whether the needed training is managerial, technical, informational, or motivational, but the steps are the same:

1. Prepare the trainee (describe the purpose of training, prerequisites, requirements, process of training, and elicit questions from learner)

2. Present the training (give an overview of the task, give examples, break down the parts of task, demonstrate the task, explain desired outcomes of task, summary)

3. Require a response (learner describes task, learner demonstrates task, learner summarizes learning)

4. Provide feedback (indicate correctness of learner response while coaching learners)

5. Evaluate performance (compare to standard and desired outcomes)

Additional individual-focused learning strategies that you might consider are:

- Peer Tutoring

- Employee Exchange

- Job Aids

- Self-Instructional Books and Articles

- Writing Assignments

CHAPTER VII

Small-Group Learning

This chapter explains how work groups and teams can be opportunities for learning. The more powerful structure for learning, however, is the true team. Katzenbach and Smith provide this definition of teams:

> . . . a small number of people with complementary skills who are committed to a common purpose, performance goals, and approach for which they hold themselves mutually accountable.

This definition suggests that teams are more dependent on organizational learning for their success. Team members learn collectively. But whether group members are working together simply because they share the same task (work group) or they are together because their success is determined by their ability to function as a cohesive, coordinated, integrated unit (team), groups can and do learn.

Group-focused organizational learning enhances the capacity of a small group (approximately two to twenty people) to act as a unit in the workplace. The members' collective know-how and know-why change the culture, behavior, and effectiveness of the group. They are both learning together and learning how to learn together.

What does it take for a group to be effective and to sustain that success over time? The key is to create an environment for optimal and continuous learning. Connectivity, defined by Marcial Losada as the number and quality of interactions among group members, is what creates this environment, and what makes high performance groups successful. Connectivity is achieved by balancing inquiry with advocacy, by focusing on others as well as on oneself, and by maintaining a high ratio of positive feedback to negative feedback.

Group learning should be linked to the goals of the group and the goals of the organization as a whole. The group discovers through its own experience how to become a more effective part of the system. This learning builds the capacity of the group to achieve high performance, which in turn helps the organization achieve its potential.

Teams that achieve high performance in the workplace go through a process of learning and change that causes them to become increasingly effective. The Drexler/Sibbet Team Performance Model is useful because it helps us relate the stages of team development that make up this process to the learning that needs to happen at each stage. These stages do not necessarily occur in order, however: Goal and role clarification (Stage 3) might occur, for example, while trust building (Stage 2) is still going on.

There are seven stages to the model:

THE DREXLER/SIBBET TEAM PERFORMANCE MODEL

Stage 1: Orientation

Group members need to understand why they are in the group, and why others are there. They need to know how they can contribute to the work of the team, and they need to believe that the team can accomplish something worthwhile.

Stage 2: Trust Building

Group members need to be able to trust the other members of the team, and need to feel trusted by them. When team members trust each other, the feedback is more open and honest. Members learn that their own risk-taking builds this trust.

Stage 3: Goal/Role Clarification

Group members need to know the specific task of the group—what is within its charge and what is outside its charge—and what each person's responsibilities are with respect to those goals. They must reach consensus on the purpose of the group and the roles of individual members before they can expect meaningful work to be done.

Stage 4: Commitment

Group members need to know how they will do their work together. They need to have a shared understanding of how decisions will be made, how resources will be used, and (probably most importantly) how dependent they are on each other to achieve the group goals.

THE DREXLER/SIBBET TEAM PERFORMANCE MODEL (continued)

Stage 5: Implementation

Group members need to have a clear picture in their minds of the overall process for achieving the team goals. They need to understand how their individual roles and responsibilities fit into this picture, and that what they are doing is aligned with what everyone else on the team is doing.

Stage 6: High Performance

Not all teams achieve high performance—only those teams that become highly interdependent, highly interdisciplinary, and creative. This transitory state of harmony, order, and flexibility is reached when all team members are working in unison toward team goals.

Stage 7: Renewal

From time to time in the life of a team, members must decide to either recommit themselves to the work of the group or no longer continue as a team. This decision is either rejuvenating to a group that still has value to its members or freeing to members who have ceased to find value in the work.

Use these stages of team development as a guide. Look for signs that a team is moving through each stage and achieving the learning that needs to occur in order to make progress toward high performance. Remind members of the work that needs to be done if they are to fully develop as a team.

CHAPTER VIII

Strategies for Small-Group Learning

Learning at the small-group level can be enhanced if specific strategies are used. (A selection of these strategies follows.) To have maximum effect, each of these strategies must be tailored to the needs of a particular group; the group members should work together to agree on goals and performance outcomes for each activity. Ask yourself: "What should the group get out of this experience, and how should this learning be applied on the job?" Orienting group members to the same goal is critical to achieving organizational learning.

Shared Vision

A shared vision is the backdrop for learning and change. When employees know where they are trying to get to, they can identify what they need to learn in order to get there. To create a shared vision, you must achieve consensus on the direction of the group and on the desired results; everyone on the team must have the same goals for the future, and be guided by the same underlying principles. Managing by shared vision is much more productive than managing by coercion.

Every member of the team must help develop the vision. Do not try to impose a vision from the top of the organization:

While top management's endorsement and financial support for the vision is important, team ownership of the vision does not occur when the vision is promulgated exclusively by top management. Employees will not feel like the vision belongs to them unless they have a say in creating it. They will not understand the reasons for organizational change or performance improvement unless they know the facts. They will not be motivated to learn unless they believe in the new direction for the organization. Provide opportunities for all group members to have input and share reactions to that input.

If some group members have a vision for the team that is not shared by others (for example, to be recognized as a superior performer in comparison to the other members of the team), they will not contribute to team learning. The group energy will be scattered and diffused like a searchlight; each member will be focused on his/her own personal situation and not that of the team. However, if everyone in the group is committed to the same long-term goals, the energy will be concentrated like a laser beam on a single target, and everyone will work and learn together.

This does not mean that everyone on the team must approach the problem in the same way. In fact, having a shared vision frees up group members to try new approaches to the problem. For example, if the shared vision is a high quality, best-in-class climate-control system for a new car that is delivered to the internal customer on-time and within budget, then each team member can contribute in his/her own way, as long as the intent is to reach the team goal.

A shared vision comes out of group consensus, where individuals feel a sense of ownership in the goals—a belief in personal responsibility for how the results are achieved.

One way to develop consensus and ownership is to hold a visioning meeting of group members. A typical visioning session includes the following elements:

1. Sharing background information about the organization, its history, its current status, the environment in which it functions, and its strategic goals

2. Achieving consensus on what the team does well, what activities have been successful, and what resources it has available for the future

3. Achieving consensus on the principles that guide the work of the team

4. Discussing how this picture of the team fits with the vision for the organization as a whole

5. Brainstorming what team members would like to see the team achieve in three, five, or ten years

6. Achieving consensus on the priority items from the brainstorm list

7. Discussing and identifying the implications for the team of working toward these goals

8. Identifying what the team needs to learn how to do and what knowledge it needs to have in order to achieve these goals

Sustaining a shared vision over time will take work. As the months and years go by, events, developments, and trends in the environment will require you to alter or remind people of the organization's mission. As employees learn and change and the makeup of the team changes, the group can lose sight of the principles and goals. It is relatively easy, for example, to commit to outstanding customer service when revenue is high and you are fully staffed. This goal is more difficult to sustain but even more critical, however, when revenue is down and the staff is overworked. Find ways to remind team members of the current vision, and periodically repeat the visioning process or at least give employees an opportunity to affirm their commitment to the vision or their desire to change the vision.

Action Learning

Action learning is learning from doing—you must intentionally engage a group in a work activity for the purpose of learning and change, have the group reflect on the process and outcomes of that activity, and then use that newfound awareness for improving the group activity.

A. Self-Directed Action Learning

What we do is often inconsistent with the values that we say we believe in—what Argyris and Schon refer to as the difference between "theory-in-use" and "espoused theory." We are often not aware of this inconsistency, however. Action learning gives us an opportunity to surface our behavior and the values underlying this behavior in relation to the group: A manager might claim to believe that all employees deserve respect and trust, yet create rules and express expectations that are different for different people. John is asked to meet with a new client by himself, but Sally is asked to team up with a co-worker when she goes to see a new client. If managers are not aware of their inconsistent behavior, they won't see the problems it creates and the confusion, frustration, and possibly, distrust others feel because of it.

Create situations that you think you can learn from. At the next team meeting you lead make it a point to learn about your leadership behavior. During the next team project, learn about your project-management behavior. In your next performance review discussion with someone you supervise, ask for feedback about your coaching skills. (You might want a peer to sit in on the session and provide the feedback, rather than asking the person you are coaching to do this.)

The self-directed action learning worksheet that follows should help you evaluate your actions.

SELF-DIRECTED ACTION LEARNING WORKSHEET

Ask yourself:

1. What do I want to learn about myself from this situation?

2. What did I want to happen? What outcome was I hoping for?

3. What actually occurred?

4. How did the other people in the situation respond to me? What did they say, and what did they do?

5. What did I think and say that might have contributed to these outcomes?

6. How was what I said or did different from what I wanted to say and do?

7. How can I get feedback on my behavior from others? Who should I ask for feedback?

B. Group Action Learning

Groups can participate in action learning as well. You and your co-workers, for example, can be brought together for a reflective discussion, perhaps led by a facilitator so that you can join in the group reflection. This facilitator should interview participants beforehand to create a learning story that is a composite of the perceptions of the interviewees. This story then becomes the focus of group reflection, as the group examines its values and beliefs in comparison to its actual behavior. New insights will come from this kind of reflective session.

Action learning can take on more importance when a group meets or interacts regularly to collectively decide how members might deal with problems or tasks they face in their work. The decision-making process itself will help increase their understanding of the situations they are in. They will learn from each other's experience.

Action learning is not just another discussion group. A learning environment must be created in which members are able to reflect on their experiences (warts and all) and learn from the mistakes, rather than explain or excuse them. Members need to be able to listen to the experiences of others and offer careful and constructive support by asking challenging questions. Group members then need to support changes in behavior as a result of action learning.

You can help a group learn from any project by using the group action learning worksheet that follows.

GROUP ACTION LEARNING WORKSHEET
1. What did we plan, and what assumptions guided our planning?
2. What took place as planned, and why?
3. What did not happen as planned and why?
4. What did we learn from items 2 and 3 above?
5. What did we learn about our assumptions?
6. What can we do the next time? (Based on what we learned, how can we get results closer to our plan?)

Continuous Measurement

The learning that takes place within teams is directly related to continuous measurement—surfacing and collecting data about the performance of the team. Data can be numbers or stories or both, as long as they are credible to the team members and other stakeholders. These data are used to assess progress and outcomes; they keep the team energized and focused on goals. Teams that do not receive this feedback will stagnate and lose energy.

The following questions will help you assess and measure your own team's progress:

1. What are our learning and performance goals, as a group?

2. Does our team have the right people and skills to achieve our goals?

3. What will we have to learn in order to be successful?

4. Does our meeting structure encourage honest interaction and cooperation?

5. Do we feel mutually respected and trusted?

6. Do we believe that we can take risks and make mistakes without penalty?

7. Are we receiving the recognition and reward that we deserve?

8. What are we learning?

9. To what extent is our team making progress toward our performance goals?

10. What is it about the structure and culture of the larger organization that is a barrier to our team's learning and development?

11. What must be changed for us to be more effective as a team? How might we create this change?

12. What have we accomplished as a team?

13. How has our team affected the larger organization?

14. How has our team contributed to the larger organization achieving its strategic goals?

What questions would you like to investigate about your team? List them here.

_____

_____

_____

_____

The right measurement strategy for you will depend on which of these questions you ask. The most common method for assessing team members' attitudes, perceptions, and self-report of behavior is a paper-and-pencil survey of those individuals. However, other kinds of data will require more useful methods, such as:

- face-to-face interviews of individual team members and people who interact with the team

- group interviews of all team members

- structured observations of team meetings

- surveys of the team's customers

- telephone or computer-aided interviews of team members

- analysis of performance indicators, as reported in the organization's records

The data-gathering should be appropriate to the situation and be directly related to the kind of information needed by the particular team for continuous improvement or accountability. For example, if you want to know how people feel about being on the team, you should interview or survey team members. If you want to know about progress in team development (for example: team formation; communication among members; meeting dynamics; problem-solving and decision-making; rewards and recognition), observe the team in action and check your observations against the observations of the team leader and team members. If you want to know the impact of the team on the organization, survey the internal customers and examine indicators of team output. But only collect data that you and others will use to improve practice; otherwise, you are just wasting time and resources and you will lose credibility with team members.

The real value of continuous assessment is in using the findings to enhance the capacity of the team to be successful and increase its impact on the larger organization. Your actions can have tremendous impact if you do the following:

- Help teams participate in, understand, and value the continuous-measurement process.

- Engage team members as much as possible in collecting and interpreting data.

- Help them learn from the data and use the data for planning purposes.

- Ask team members:

  - What does the data say about the team's performance?

  - What does the data say about resource needs?

- How should the team change the way it functions, given the data?

- How can the team make sure that it meets its goals?

- What information should be communicated to the wider organization?

- Help the team **learn how to learn** from continuous assessment.

Dialogue

Dialogue is learning through conversation. It is a form of conversation in which you try to understand the other person's point of view, rather than convince that person of yours. Listen to each other, surface underlying assumptions and beliefs, and weave connections among ideas. You are not looking for solutions at this point, and agreement is not important. What is important is to listen to all the ideas and opinions expressed and find clarity in the meaning behind the words.

The process requires us to step outside our typical patterns of behavior in conversations, and open up to the thoughts, ideas, and feelings of others. You want shared meaning; in its purest form, it is the nature of the interaction within a conversation, rather than the positions people hold about a topic, that is most important.

Dialogue can also be used intentionally in a group in order to achieve shared meaning about a particular issue or idea. It can be used as a process for finding common ground among people who typically are in conflict with one another. The first step in helping people use dialogue is to help them see the difference between debate, which is the common approach to conversation, and dialogue, which requires a radical departure from what most of us do normally. The chart on page 70 explains the difference between debate and dialogue.

Three distinctive features characterize dialogue, according to Daniel Yankelovich's *The Magic of Dialogue*:

1. Equality and the absence of coercive influences

In the context of the dialogue, all participants must be treated equally. Superior or coercive positions in the workplace or otherwise outside of the dialogue context should not be brought into the dialogue. Participants must feel free to express themselves and should not have to screen their comments because of fear that they will be judged by others or overtly or covertly punished. During a dialogue session, do not use your position in the organizational hierarchy to try to

DIFFERENCE BETWEEN DEBATE AND DIALOGUE

DEBATE	DIALOGUE
Assuming that there is a right answer, and you have it	Assuming that many people have pieces of the answer, and that together they can craft a new solution
Combative; participants attempt to prove the other side wrong	Collaborative; participants work together toward common understanding
It's about winning	It's about exploring common ground
Listening to find flaws and make counter-arguments	Listening to understand, find meaning and agreement
Defending assumptions as truth	Revealing assumptions for re-evaluation
Critiquing the other side's position	Re-examining all positions
Defending one's own views against those of others	Admitting that others' thinking can improve on one's own
Searching for flaws and weaknesses in others' positions	Searching for strengths and value in others' positions
Seeking a conclusion or vote that ratifies your position	Discovering new options, not seeking closure

Developed by Mark Gerzon.

70

influence others; by the same token, do not let what is said during a dialogue influence decisions about individuals outside of the dialogue.

2. Listening with empathy

This refers to a commitment to try to understand another person's thoughts and feelings *from that person's point of view.* Empathic listening requires us to pay total attention to what the other person is saying, and even more importantly, to what that person is trying to communicate by what is being said. This is a difficult skill to master and it will take a great deal of practice, but when real listening and empathy are present among participants in a group, the conversation becomes richer and more meaningful.

3. Bringing assumptions into the open

Surface the assumptions behind the issue but do not judge the rightness or wrongness of these assumptions. For example, one of the members of a group might express the opinion that the designated team leader should be responsible for making sure that the work of the group gets done. In another setting, you might react to this comment by thinking that the person is refusing to accept his/her own responsibility. In a dialogue, however, you must acknowledge his/her right to hold the opinion. Try to draw him/her out about the meaning of the belief. Discover how you and others can learn from this perspective.

The art of listening with empathy, described in an earlier section of this book, is the key to dialogue. You cannot learn all that another person has to contribute unless you listen fully to what that person is communicating. This means blocking out those conversations in our heads about what we agree with and what we disagree with, what we like about the person and what we do not like, and how we can convince that person of our position on an issue. In the space that is left ask yourself:

- What is she (he) trying to communicate to me?

- What does she really mean by the words?

- What are the feelings that go with the words?

- What do I need to ask her in order to more fully understand what she is saying?

- Am I making any assumptions about what she is saying that I should ask about?

- How does what she is saying connect to what others have said in the group so far?

Here are some basic guidelines for dialogues with members of a small group:

GUIDELINES FOR SMALL-GROUP DIALOGUES

1. **Hear from everyone in the group.** Discover what you have in common. Discuss the challenges that are faced by everyone in the group.

2. **Recognize that the knowledge and experience that everyone has is sufficient to explore the question.**

3. **Create a spirit of inquiry.** Stimulate curiosity and questioning.

4. **Acknowledge that it is normal to feel both comfort and discomfort in reaction to what others say.**

5. **Accept and acknowledge that no one has the right answer.**

6. **Do not try to prove or persuade.** Offer your perspective and look for connections to what others have said.

Reflection

Reflection is putting up a mirror to yourself and the people and events around you, and learning from what you see. Three kinds of reflection lead to group learning according to Killion and Hamson: (1) reflection-on-action (looking back on what happened); (2) reflection-in-action (examining the situation while you are in it); and (3) reflection-for-action (focusing on what was learned and how that learning can be used in the future). Questions that can guide each of these kinds of reflection in groups are listed on the following worksheet.

WORKSHEET FOR GROUP REFLECTION

Reflection-on-action:

- How does the group feel about the situation?

- What went well?

- What did not go as well as we expected?

- What options did we consider as we selected the behavior/action?

- What option did we choose?

- How did we know that what we chose to do would be best in this situation? What did we base that on (i.e., theory, experience, intuition)?

- How did we know that another behavior/action would not be appropriate?

- What made this situation unusual?

- What might we have done differently?

Learning History

Learning histories are like highly structured group reflections. They provide an opportunity to look back on an important

WORKSHEET FOR GROUP REFLECTION

Reflection-in-action:

■ What cues from the group do we see that tell us how they are responding to our behaviors/actions?

■ What assumptions or inferences are we making?

■ What options are available? What are the possible consequences of each? What will work best in this situation?

■ What principles/theories are guiding us?

■ What is unique about this situation?

■ What level of direction/specificity/structure is best here?

Reflection-for-action:

■ What did we learn that we can apply in other situations?

■ How did we alter our knowledge, theories, or attitudes as a result of this experience?

■ What did we learn from this situation that confirms our expectations?

■ What will we remember from this situation?

■ If we find ourselves in a similar situation again, how will we behave?

event or series of events in the life of the group and to learn collectively from successes and failures. The focus could be a team's development of a new product, a major change effort such as a work group switching from cost accounting to activity-based accounting, or the strategic planning process of an administrative team.

As recommended by Kleiner and Roth, the key stakeholders (team members and others who are affected by the work of the team) in the event are interviewed regarding the facts of the event and their reactions and actions in response to the event. Typically, these interviews are put in the form of a written narrative in two-column format: The right-hand column contains the story as told by the people who were interviewed, using direct quotes as much as possible. The left-hand column contains an analysis by a group of "learning historians" who identify themes in the content, comment on the meaning of what was said in the right-hand column, pose questions for the reader to consider, and surface undiscussible issues suggested by the story. An example of this narrative follows.

EXAMPLE OF A LEARNING HISTORY: LEADERS FIND NEW ROLES

These leaders acknowledge their leadership abilities and responsibilities, yet recognize that because the way decisions have to be made is changing, they have to modify their power behaviors with subordinates. Deep shifts in their own attitudes are the starting point.

Column A: Contains learning historians' summary and analysis of what workers said in Column B	Column B: What stakeholders have to say about the event; contains information about their reactions and response
Learning to share decision-making with subordinates is one of the most difficult changes for leaders to make.	**Operations Manager 3:** I know personally just how traumatic it has been for me to make the necessary changes, to take off my old management hat. They literally threw me out of the first meetings of the operation-level teams. I said that I was sitting in on the meetings to help the new teams, but they finally just told me, "We don't want you in here; you're not helping us."

Provided by Ann Thomas.

EXAMPLE OF A LEARNING HISTORY (continued)

I knew it, but it was hard to let go because I had the information and the answers for them. To let them develop that themselves was very hard.

Senior Manager 2: As leaders, we were accustomed to making decisions. We had some very, very painful moments while we learned how to act like team members and learned how not to make decisions for others. I was probably the worst of the bunch. In the beginning people would say, "She's never going to be able to do this." I didn't think I was going to be able to do it either.

There were these 200 people around and they wanted instant answers. Somebody would ask me a question in the hall and I knew immediately what I thought they should do, which was what I would have said to them six months ago. Now though, I had to say to them, "Let me get with the leadership team and I'll get back to you."

EXAMPLE OF A LEARNING HISTORY (continued)

Operations Manager 3: We put a cross-level, operations/human resources team together to implement the change. As the management-level representatives, we explained that we considered everyone else on the team as peers. It was culture shock for the hourly people, though; they were very uncomfortable with managers as peers.

A key event happened after several months of meetings. The management-level team members, including myself, had gone off and hammered out a vision for the team effort. When we brought it into the team meeting, one of the hourly guys finally said: "If you really want us on this team, I'll tell you what I think: What you've written is BS. No one is going to believe it . . . it's just management rhetoric."

We managers looked at each other and realized that we had taken over. That was a breaking point. After that, we rewrote the vision as a whole team and went forward from there.

EXAMPLE OF A LEARNING HISTORY (continued)

Sharing information across levels is another behavior change that is important in moving change forward.	**Operations Manager 3:** Managers, including myself, don't always realize that the only difference between ourselves and our employees is the amount of information we control. It's not a difference in intelligence. Given the same information, the teams are going to make the same decisions as would the manager. Teams may take a little longer because their base is not as experienced, but they do make the same decision. The resistance is in the manager letting go, giving them the information, and waiting for the decision. In our teams that are really working, the manager has let go and the coaches are really coaching.
Positive encouragement helps people find new meaning and satisfaction in the work they do.	**Senior Manager 1:** It's me providing a vision and getting buy-in from those people, but it isn't just me doing it—I always say I don't do much of anything; I stimulate others.

EXAMPLE OF A LEARNING HISTORY (concluded)

	Any meaningful change in an organization requires a vision and expectations, and when things get sketchy, requires us to be persistent with those expectations. I just keep talking about them. It's great to watch people change their behavior patterns and recognize their abilities—abilities they didn't know they had. For instance, I saw people who probably had never seen the inside of a math class stand up in front of a group and talk about statistics.
The personal credibility of the leader assumes more importance during transformation.	**Operations Manager 2:** When you lead people, you do it through personal credibility. You know you're not doing all the work, but you're a critical enough piece of the machine that if you fall out, the whole thing comes to an end. You have to have this unwavering focus and discipline, and you really have to believe in what you're doing.

Additional strategies that you might consider to facilitate small-group learning are:

- Town Meetings

- Focus Groups

- Simulations

- Communities of Practice

CHAPTER IX

Whole-Organization Learning

How can you help the whole organization learn how to take effective action? First, by helping everyone in the organization understand the dynamic interaction of all of its various parts, and then by reflecting on the significance of that understanding for building the effectiveness of the whole organization.

To learn, we need to feel the psychological safety and support of a community. We act like a learning community when there is a feeling of connectedness among the members, when everyone considers themselves to be members of that community, when there is continuity between generations (eventually new members add to or replace the knowledge of old members), and when there is a common purpose and shared aspirations. Creating a sense of community is the foundation for whole-organization learning.

Therefore, the challenge is to change an organization into a learning community. To do this we must attend to the structure of the organization. Is it a structure that fosters community in the sense of connectedness, membership, continuity, common purpose, and shared aspirations? For example, a rigid hierarchy does not promote a sense of connectedness among employees.

The boxes and lines on an organizational chart say more about where the connections are not than where they are.

Organizational structures, by design, determine the results. If we want to achieve different results, we must change the organizational structure. So the question for you is, *How can you get a large (or not so large), complex organization to understand how its structure inhibits the achievement of optimal results, and then, how do we get it to agree on high leverage changes to improve outcomes?*

Our natural tendency is to analyze—to understand complex entities by separating them into small parts in our thinking and then to make assumptions (informed or not) about the meaning of one of those parts. We try to explain stock-market performance by looking at interest rates. We try to predict U.S. elections from a political party's position on trade with China. We critique the performance of U.S. public schools by using SAT scores as the indicator of success. If only the world was that simple! We cannot truly understand and learn from these phenomena unless we consider the dynamic interactions of many factors affecting human behavior.

The complexity of the whole organization is likely to be overwhelming unless you use a coherent learning-based approach to achieve this understanding. The strategies that lead to whole-organization learning focus on the integration rather than the separation of people, units, and information.

CHAPTER X

Strategies for Whole-Organization Learning

Causal Loop

One approach to analyzing and understanding the complexity in our organizations is to create a graphical representation, or map, of the elements of the system, describing how and when they relate to each other. One tool for mapping these relationships is the causal loop, a diagram that tells a story about the situation. You can use the drawing to explain the dynamic interdependencies that influence behavior in your organization; when you do this with groups of employees, the barriers to improvement will become explicit and resistance will drop because people will realize that this dynamic interaction is due to the structure of the organization rather than because of some failure in them personally. The focus will shift to solutions rather than blame, which makes causal loops good tools for learning *how to learn*, rather than simply learning how to solve an archetypal problem.

Drawing appropriate causal loops takes practice. You will need to learn the language of the loops—the symbols and the meaning of the elements of the drawings. You will also need to learn how to facilitate a discussion so that you surface the stories that describe what the loops represent.

The causal loop below tells the story of team risk taking. The upper loop indicates that by praising effort from the start (as opposed to praising results), employees will be more likely to accept risk-taking behavior, which leads to more experimenting and more learning, and more praise for trying. The lower loop indicates that when experimenting results in a negative reaction from others (such as critical comments, reassignments, loss of resources), defensive responses will increase and people will develop a fear of failing. This fear makes them less willing to experiment and take creative chances.

Team Risk-Taking Causal Loop

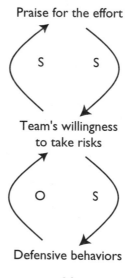

Praise for the effort

S   S

Team's willingness
to take risks

O   S

Defensive behaviors

Benchmarking

The Xerox Corp. is credited with being the first to use benchmarking as a strategic tool. The company found out that it could learn much from the practices of other organizations and from the process of comparing its organization to others. This is true for all of us, whether we're comparing one internal unit to another or comparing our processes to those of other organizations who do something especially well. Xerox labeled these activities *benchmarking*.

However, simply visiting another company to see how it assembles a product, solves customer problems, works with its business partners, or conducts its meetings is not the kind of benchmarking that will result in organizational learning. To really learn, you must take your organization through a process of: (1) Self-assessment; (2) Examining what is done by another organization; (3) Using that information to plan change at home; and (4) Supporting that change through training and development activities.

The key to this whole process is to do a thorough self-assessment up front where you learn very specifically what needs to be changed. This means collecting enough data to make you confident that you fully understand the depth and breadth of the problem. (It is not enough to know that the machines on the shop floor are breaking down frequently.) If you try to benchmark with only a superficial understanding of the problem, you will not know what organization to select for benchmarking, what to look for in that organization, or how to apply the alternative approach. You also will not be able to gain the support and acceptance of those who have to implement the changes in your unit. You need to know which machines are breaking down and under what conditions, who is involved in maintenance and how are they handling it, what suggestions they have for improvement, and what factors are contributing to the breakdowns, such as the maintenance schedule, the production process, the capacity of employees to maintain the machines, the maintenance budget provided by the finance department, the quality of the machines, and the plant floor environment (too cold, too hot, too dirty, too dry, etc.). If you do not know that the environment is part of the problem, you might not ask the benchmark organization that you select about maintaining the quality of air in the workplace. And the critical question you need to ask during the self-assessment phase is, "Should we be doing this process in the first place?"

Before you even embark on a benchmarking project, prepare the organization for learning and change. Leaders and workers must accept that they are not the best in everything and that they have something to learn, especially from others outside the organization. Prepare them for using the information that you collect, and be sure they understand that they might have to change some things and train people in the new processes. Do not begin raising expectations that things will improve before you help people develop the skills, knowledge, and attitudes they need to make the necessary changes.

World Café

The World Café process was designed by Whole System Associates to create the conditions conducive for conversation among all the members of a large group. Recognizing that collaborative learning is an essential aspect of a sustainable community, the World Café is a tool to help an entire community collaborate for the purpose of learning. The World Café creates a network of conversations around questions that lead the group to a shared understanding. It is a way of sharing knowledge and accessing the collective intelligence of the community.

Almost any number of people can participate in this activity. The only restrictions on size are the size of the space you have in which to meet, the number of people you have to assist in facilitating the event, and your capacity for collecting and summarizing the information that is collected during the event.

The conversation is based on the principles and processes of dialogue: Participants listen to each other, surface underlying assumptions and beliefs, and achieve greater shared understanding without the pressure for solutions. Agreement is not important, but listening to all ideas and opinions is. You should be concerned about clarity of meaning, not the facts. Begin the conversation with the one question that, if answered, will make the most difference to the total group.

The World Café's success is due to the following characteristics:

- Hospitable Space
  There must be a space for conversation in small groups that is informal, inviting, and safe for everyone (usually similar to café-style seating, with small tables and four to six chairs around each table).

- Questions That Matter
  The question must be powerful enough to motivate people to seek collective insight.

- Spirit of Discovery
  The conversations are more like dialogue than normal, everyday discussion; participants give information and ask questions without trying to convince someone else to take a particular position on an issue.

- Shared Listening
  Participants listen for connections and themes that run throughout the conversation; these connections and themes are written or drawn on paper at the center of each table and left behind as participants change tables several times. A host stays at the table to provide continuity for the next group that comes to the table.

- Awareness of Connections
  Connections are made among the conversations that occur at each table for each table group, and then among all of the tables.

External Threats to the System

The threat of total system breakdown provides an opportunity for significant organizational learning. Margaret Wheatley provides us with suggested actions for learning that leaders can take in situations that threaten total organization failure.

1. Engage the whole system. Only participation can save you.

2. Keep expanding the system. Ask "Who else should be involved?"

3. Create abundant information and circulate it through existing and new channels (dedicated Web sites or intranets).

4. Develop simple reporting systems that can generate information quickly and broadcast it easily.

5. Develop quality relationships as a top priority; trust is the greatest asset.

6. Support collaboration; competition destroys capacity.

7. Demolish boundaries and territories; push for openness everywhere.

8. Focus on creating new, streamlined systems. There is no going back!

These suggestions (more like imperatives) offered in the context of potential large-scale system failure are relevant to any organization that has complex interdependencies within and between its internal and external communities—one that is faced with a problem that affects that total system: loss of a key leader; major loss of market share; core product failures; large revenue shifts; large cost shifts; significant new government regulations; or environmental catastrophes such as a fire, an earthquake, or a flood that suddenly destroys units of business operations.

Appreciative Inquiry

The basic idea behind appreciative inquiry, as proposed by David Cooperrider, is to make everyone aware of the positive experiences and successes of the organization. Rather than analyzing problems and trying to identify what is wrong with the organization, which is the most common approach, the focus of appreciative inquiry is on what is right and how you can learn from and build on these strengths.

A three-step process prepares you for appreciative inquiry in a large-group meeting:

Step One:
Choose the topic and put it in positive terms.

Step Two:
Create questions that will stimulate participants to report positive examples.

Step Three:
Ask the questions of everyone who is a source of the information. Keep in mind that asking questions is a kind of intervention into the life of the organization, so err on the side of inclusion, and listen carefully to the answers.

Once these preparatory steps have been completed, you can begin the 4-D process:

1. Discovery: Report the stories from the preparatory steps, and discuss their significance for the future of the organization.

2. Dream: Discuss what everyone wants the organization to look like in five years; come to consensus on a vision, mission, and strategic goals.

3. Design: Using the vision for the future, decide on a set of driving concepts and principles by which the organization will operate.

4. Destiny: Support application and sustain what was decided in the first three phases.

Four statements guide this strategy:

- Appreciate **What Is**
- Imagine **What Might B**e
- Determine **What Should Be**
- Create **What Will Be**

Large-Scale Learning Events

What if you could get your whole organization, or a large part of it, together in one location to experience self-discovery, teamwork, and problem-solving, and to create a shared vision of the future? Wouldn't this be a great opportunity for learning? This is the purpose of a number of event-driven large-group strategies. What these various strategies have in common is a very large number of employees in a time-limited event participating in new ways that challenge the bureaucratic, hierarchical, command-and-control cultures that are typical of the participants' organizations.

For several of these designs, the only factors that limit the number of participants are the size of the room, the logistics of bringing that many people together at the same time, and the number and capability of the facilitators. For example, the "Whole-Scale Change" design was used in one event for the 2000 employees of an automobile manufacturing plant. The cavernous rooms of a downtown convention center had to be rented for this three-day process, which included whole-group and small-group activities.

Some of the other large-scale designs that have proved to be effective and the people who have developed them are:

- Future Search—Marvin Weisbord
- Preferred Futuring—Ronald Lippitt and Lawrence L. Lippitt
- Whole-Scale Change—Kathleen Dannemiller
- Open Space Technology—Harrison Owen
- The Conference Model—Emily M. Axelrod and Richard H. Axelrod

(For more information on these innovators, see the Resources Section.)

PART THREE

What are the organizational structures that support learning?

Learning is supported at the individual, small-group, and whole-organization levels by certain aspects of the organization's environment that encourage surfacing, noticing, gathering, sharing, and applying new knowledge. These conditions are not always readily visible or measurable, but they always affect organizational learning. The culture of the organization, the ways in which people communicate with each other, the ways in which people lead, knowledge-management, how the organization evaluates its performance, and the physical environment of workspaces, all help determine how well learning is sustained over time.

CHAPTER XI

Culture of the Organization

Schein has defined culture as the values, basic assumptions, beliefs, expected behaviors, and norms of an organization; the aspects of an organization that affect how people think, feel, and act. Members of an organization have a shared sense of culture that operates mostly unconsciously and that is manifested in every aspect of organizational life in subtle and not-so-subtle ways. From the rituals of celebration to how decisions are made, culture is made up of the artifacts and the actions of the members. It is passed on to new employees in what they are told and what they observe in the behavior, symbols, and documents around them.

Continuous organizational learning depends on a culture of learning throughout the organization. Your role is to help shape this culture of learning. Make the pursuit of learning everyone's responsibility, from top management down to the line worker.

Organizations are replete with examples of how culture does not support learning: employees pass around stories (true or not) about co-workers who were forced out of the company because they tried something new. Managers tell their subordinates to develop new skills, but then chastise them for being away from work at a training event. They reward employees through compensation or perks for "making their numbers" at the end of the month, but do not reward them for engaging in cross-functional team problem-solving. They reward individual, but not team results, and assign teams to conduct research on the quality of a product or service and then fail to use the findings and recommendations. Daniel Tobin had this to say about how leaders can create a learning culture:

> Successful companies encourage employee learning, through training programs and, even more so, by enabling and facilitating the exchange of knowledge and ideas and by empowering employees to try new ideas to help improve their own and the company's performance. If a new idea doesn't work out, the employee is rewarded for a thoughtful, well-conceived attempt at improvement—not punished for failing. Managers in these organizations coach employees and reinforce their learning to ensure that new ideas are properly applied to the job to add value to the employee's work.

CREATE AND MAINTAIN A CULTURE THAT IS CONDUCIVE TO LEARNING

■ Make highly visible and dramatic changes that are symbolic, as well as substantive, of a learning culture in the organization.

■ Make sure that values in action are consistent with espoused values of learning. Initiate this conversation with your employees.

■ Assess and compare the perceived current culture with the desired learning culture.

■ Develop a shared plan for what the organization must do to move from the current culture to the desired learning culture.

■ Allow employees to dedicate time to formal and informal learning that will enhance their capacity to do their work effectively.

■ Develop learning events that are explicitly linked to the strategic goals of the organization.

■ Create ceremonies that give recognition to learning by individuals and teams.

■ Make the artifacts of learning visible to employees, such as a library, spaces for formal and informal conversations among employees, benefits that support education, and computer access to just-in-time information.

■ Provide feedback to individuals and groups that use learning applied to organizational capacity as one indicator of success.

CHAPTER XII

Communication

Often what we think to be good interpersonal communication is actually a barrier to learning. Managers tend to say and do things to keep morale high, to be considerate and positive, and to not open the Pandora's box of problems. But in effect, as Argyris points out, they are preventing employees from confronting problems and learning from mistakes. Managers' behavior often discourages questioning about the underlying values and rationale for organizational decisions and practices. For the sake of harmony, bad practice goes unexamined. It is understandable. People do not want to experience embarrassment, loss of control, tension, and unhappiness in the workplace. However, the cost is enormous. The organization does not learn from its own behavior.

To avoid these organizational defensive routines, ask the hard questions and encourage others to do the same. Confront the hard facts and sensitive feelings. Ask others, "What goes on in this organization that prevents us from questioning these practices and getting them corrected or eliminated?" and "What can we do to bring about a change?"

But be careful not to punish people for being open and honest when you hear their responses! This is easy to do withou realizing it, so be on your guard. If an employee takes a risk and tries something new and fails, focus on what was learned rather than on what went wrong. If an employee challenges a practice that you started or you support, do not immediately try to think of reasons why the employee's thinking is wrong—instead, try to find ways in which you can incorporate the employee's ideas. If an employee asks, "Why does the company continue to offer a service that is losing money?" Do not say that it is because management wants it done. Find out the rationale, and report this back to the employee. Focusing on what went wrong or trying to poke holes in someone's ideas and shifting blame are all examples of reactions that feel like punishment to the person on the receiving end.

Keep in mind the principles of dialogue presented earlier in this book: Try to understand the other person's point of view, rather than convince that person of your position. Listen to each other, surface underlying assumptions and beliefs, and weave connections among ideas. Look for clarity. Do not look for solutions. Agreement is not important. What is important is listening to all ideas and opinions.

Once you fully understand the employee's ideas and suggestions, demonstrate that you value this openness and honesty by acting on what the employee has said. Communicate back to the employee that his/her ideas and suggestions influenced your thinking or were part of a discussion among managers, or maybe actually changed the practice. Acting on the suggestion is not as important as letting the employee know that you value the comments and that the lines of communication are still open between you.

CHAPTER XIII

Leadership

What do people mean by *leadership*? Most employees are not looking for a leader like Gandhi or Churchill. For the most part, they just want someone who will help them be successful without a lot of pain. Unfortunately, what they usually get is someone who gets a lot of things done, but who does not help individuals, teams, and the whole organization learn.

A hierarchical, command-and-control leadership style is still predominant in all types of organizations regardless of organizational values and mission. Rummler and Brache contend that it is effective in certain situations, but when it comes to organizational learning, it is usually a barrier. This style closes off vital input from the various parts of the organization as well as from outside. Hierarchical leaders put energy into maintaining the lines of authority and communication represented by the organizational chart, and do not generally seek and use information from inside and outside of their functional area.

The "command and control" leadership style was effective at a time when stability was valued more than change, loyalty valued more than quality, similarities valued more than differences, and individuality valued more than teamwork. It has dominated management behavior since the Industrial Revolution, and still dominates management today. However, it's a new workplace out there, and what is needed particularly for organizational learning, is a different kind of leader.

For leadership to make a difference in organizational learning, it must be linked to the outcomes that the particular organization needs for success. These outcomes are specific performance improvements of the individual, the team, or the organization. This conceptual link between leadership and results for the organization should be made apparent to all stakeholders. These questions will help you make this link between leadership and results:

CRITICAL LEADERSHIP QUESTIONS

Ask yourself and others the following five basic questions. The order of these questions is critical.

1. What are the long-term outcomes that will indicate that the organization is successful? (Businesses often express this in terms of profit, market share, and return to stockholders; nonprofits express this in terms of revenue, community needs that are being met, and the number of participants.)
2. What are the short-term business objectives that will lead to these long-term outcomes? (Businesses often express this in terms of reduced costs, quality, and safety; nonprofits often express this in terms of reputation, community access, and customer satisfaction.)
3. What work processes need to be improved to achieve these business objectives?
4. What are the critical job tasks that leaders in this organization must do to improve these work processes?
5. What knowledge, skills, and attitudes do leaders in this organization need to perform these critical job tasks?

WHAT IS LEADERSHIP FOR ORGANIZATIONAL LEARNING?

"...We suggest that leadership that is developed at the upper end is considered more transformational. Such leadership would involve establishing one's beliefs and values and being consistent with them; determining a course for change in the future and articulating it as a vision; stimulating co-workers and oneself to challenge traditional ways of thinking; and developing oneself and others to the highest levels of potential." (Kellogg Leadership Studies Project, *Transformational Leadership Working Papers*, October 1997)

"Leaders are truly transformational when they increase awareness of what is right, good, important, and beautiful; when they help to elevate followers' needs for achievement and self-actualization; when they foster in followers higher moral maturity; and when they move followers to go beyond their self-interests for the good of their group, organization, or society." (Bernard M. Bass, *The Ethics of Transformational Leadership*)

"All effective leaders ... know four simple things: 1. The only definition of a leader is someone who has followers. Some people are thinkers. Some are prophets. Both roles are important and badly needed. But without followers, there can be no leaders. 2. An effective leader is not someone who is loved or admired. He or she is someone whose followers do the right things. Popularity is not leadership. Results are. 3. Leaders are highly visible. They therefore set examples. 4. Leadership is not rank, privileges, titles, or money. It is responsibility." (Peter F. Drucker, *The Leader of the Future*, 1996, p. xii)

"Leadership is about creating, day by day, a domain in which we and those around us continually deepen our understanding of reality and are able to participate in shaping the future. This, then, is the deeper territory of leadership—collectively listening to what is wanting to emerge in the world, and then having the courage to do what is required." (Joseph Jaworski, *Synchronicity*, 1996, p. 182)

WHAT MAKES A GOOD LEADER?

FedEx looks for the following nine personal characteristics in its leaders:

1. Charisma: Instills faith, respect, and trust. Conveys a strong sense of mission.

2. Individual Consideration: Coaches, advises, and teaches people who need it.

3. Intellectual Stimulation: Gets others to use reasoning and evidence, rather than unsupported opinion.

4. Courage: Willing to stand up for ideas, even if they are unpopular.

5. Dependability: Follows through and keeps commitments.

6. Flexibility: Functions effectively in changing environments. Changes course when the situation warrants it.

7. Integrity: Does what is morally and ethically right.

8. Judgment: Reaches sound and objective evaluations of alternative courses of action through logic, analysis, and comparison.

9. Respect for Others: Honors and does not belittle the opinions or work of other people, regardless of their status or position.

These are also the characteristics of a leader who facilitates organizational learning.

CHAPTER XIV

Knowledge-Management

Much knowledge in organizations goes unshared and unused. I am sure you have had the experience of working on a project for several months, only to discover that a co-worker down the hall from you completed a similar project last year. Perhaps the new service your company is providing to its customers was tried by a former employee (now with a competitor) who left no record of the development, implementation, and results. Perhaps you were asked to make recommendations regarding a new business process, but you do not know how to find out what has been done before and who is knowledgeable about this type of process.

Knowledge-management is about transferring information and best practices from one part of an organization to another part. O'Dell and Grayson phrased it this way:

> Knowledge management is . . . a conscious strategy of getting the right knowledge to the right people at the right time and helping people share and put information into action in ways that strive to improve organizational performance.

This means managing both human and technological sources of information, and turning this information into knowledge and getting it to people when and where they need it. The generic steps in the knowledge-management process are: create, identify, collect, organize, share, adapt, and use internal knowledge and best practices. Effort is not wasted on reinventing the wheel and unnecessary errors. When this happens the whole organization gets smarter.

Two kinds of knowledge exist in organizations, says Ikujiro Nonaka. Tacit knowledge is the informal and uncodified learning that resides primarily in the minds of employees. Explicit knowledge is formal and codified; it resides in paper documents and computer files, and can be accessed by employees, assuming they know where to find this information.

Create opportunities for your employees to share both tacit and explicit knowledge with other employees who can benefit from the information and experience. Encourage the experienced employees to describe their successes and learnings from similar projects. These learnings can take the form of subjective insights, intuition, or hunches. By making all of this information explicit, others can test the validity of the conclusions.

Make information technology part of your knowledge-management system. The computer network and company intranet provide a place to store and retrieve information. Hire a professional librarian to manage the system. They usually have the training to evaluate, store, and retrieve information and knowledge, and to use the latest technology to serve the information needs of your customers. Make sure that this person has a background in library reference and experience helping people use information databases in a corporate setting.

Simply asking people to share information will not be enough. Provide a clear vision for knowledge-management in the organization. Help employees understand how knowledge-management will help them achieve their strategic goals. Create incentives for transferring information across departments. Provide opportunities for employees to meet to share their experiences on similar projects and what they learned from these efforts. Show employees that non-original ideas are valued. Make it easy for employees to enter project information in a database that is accessible to all. Provide resources for gathering and using the organization's information.

Do not assume that just because you have cross-functional work groups or teams that knowledge and best practices are being shared among departments. Group members have to see knowledge and best-practice sharing as their responsibility and that it is essential to success. Also, you have to create an environment where people feel safe in divulging what they have learned from prior experiences.

Training and knowledge-management should go hand in hand. Training is one way of conveying the organization's knowledge to large numbers of employees and an important aspect of the knowledge-management system. Ask trainers to design opportunities for participants to share their experience and lessons learned. Whether it is a management-development seminar or a computer software class, participants should be given an opportunity to discuss their experiences related to the topic. For example, in a project-management seminar, participants should share with each other what they have learned about effective and ineffective ways to work with suppliers and other external resources. Not only will this sharing contribute to the transfer of knowledge throughout the organization, but participants will feel better about their involvement in the seminar.

The use of information technology should only become a focus after you are clear about goals, values, and barriers. New computer technology is making knowledge-management cheaper and more efficient all the time. The Internet and company intranets are powerful tools that are revolutionizing the sharing of information. Enterprise-training software is promising to create a single database for all employee learning.

But simply installing this technology is not the complete answer to knowledge-management. Much explicit knowledge can be stored and retrieved through computer systems, but tacit knowledge must be tapped in other ways. Some solutions are based in technology (intranet, on-line libraries, databases) and some solutions are based in human interaction. Both are important. Explicit knowledge can be posted at a Web site, but tacit knowledge is not present until people meet and start sharing their thoughts and experiences with one another.

Increasing the flow of information is not difficult. The challenge is to increase the flow and use of knowledge.

WAYS TO INCREASE FLOW AND USE OF KNOWLEDGE

- Formal training programs that provide new information, teach skills, and shape attitudes and beliefs.

- Individual tutoring of employees by experts or co-workers who have experience and information needed by those employees.

- Publishing, marketing, and dissemination of documents that communicate organizational knowledge in an interesting and useful way.

- Formal presentations of information to groups and teams throughout the organization that include conversations about the meaning and application of that information.

- Coaching managers on using new knowledge to help them achieve their goals.

- Being a mentor to employees (especially new employees) and guiding them through the process of finding, evaluating, and applying the information they need to do their jobs effectively.

- Using various kinds of information technology, such as document databases; discussion databases; Internet and intranet links to experts; document exchange; performance-support systems; help desks; and data analysis software, to achieve business goals.

CHAPTER XV

Evaluation

Evaluation is essential to learning. Our society emphasizes right and wrong, good and bad, worthy and unworthy, winning and losing. Because of this, we tend to think that evaluation is about placing blame. Not true: the true significance of evaluation in organizations is that it provides information that will result in improved performance.

Evaluation means looking for indicators of progress toward and achievement of strategic goals, and understanding what it is about the learning process that is helping employees improve and sustain their performance over time. You must identify aspects of the organization that are barriers to learning and high performance, because this is how organizations change and improve themselves.

All members of the organization need to be continually asking:

- What are we doing?
- How well are we doing it?
- How can it be improved?

These reflective questions should be applied to all of the activities, processes, and systems within the organization.

Involve representatives of key stakeholder groups (employees, customers, clients, suppliers, business partners, and others who have a vested interest in the performance of the organization), because they are more likely to use the results for their own learning if they are involved from the outset. Collaborate with them to decide what should be evaluated, what questions should be asked, and how the information will be used once it is collected.

Evaluation of organizational learning measures the interaction of each element of the learning process. We want to know what elements of the system affect learning and how this learning results in enhanced organizational capacity to be successful.

Evaluation measures do not have to be rigorous, in fact, the simpler the better. The point is to collect data (numbers, descriptions, stories) that help the stakeholders understand the progress that employees and the organization are making toward business goals. These stakeholders need to know what is working well and what should be changed; if, for example, the managers of a manufacturing line are presented with evidence that their behavior is a barrier to the performance improvement of employees on that line and they don't allow trainees to apply their new learning, they might decide to change their behavior and support performance improvement. Until they have this feedback, they are unlikely to change.

Once you decide what needs to be evaluated and why, and how you will use the information in the organization, then you are ready to select the appropriate method of measurement. For example, if you are trying to develop a high performance team, you might want to:

- Survey team members about their attitudes toward

teamwork

- Interview team members about the effectiveness of communication among team members

- Observe the team members in action to assess how they work together

- Survey the team's internal and external customers about their perceptions of the team's effectiveness

- Examine team products for indicators of quality

Managers throughout the organization are important partners in the application of these methods and in the utilization of the information. The results of these measures should be reported to other managers who can use the information for process-improvement purposes. By bringing other managers into the performance-improvement process, you build a sense of organization-wide ownership and commitment to performance-improvement. The responsibility for learning and change shifts to the people in the organization who have significant influence on the organization's success.

Measure the outcomes of the learning process. Any learning process has short-term outcomes that show progress towards strategic goals and long-term outcomes that show the impact of the learning on the organization. These outcomes include:

- New employee skills, knowledge, and attitudes

- Achievement of job behavior objectives

- Achievement of job output objectives

- Achievement of business process objectives

- Achievement of department/unit goals

- Achievement of business strategic goals

The following suggestions will make the evaluation of organizational learning useful to you and to your organization:

- Involve internal customers in deciding what to measure and how to measure it.

  Ask them what they want to know and why. Ask them for their thoughts about the data-collection methods that you are recommending. Ask them to help pilot these methods to see if they will produce the information that you need. Often a workshop format that allows these stakeholders to work together as a group is useful. This process of answering measurement questions with input from key stakeholders can be more valuable to developing a high performance organization than the actual data that are collected.

- Choose the method of measurement only after deciding what to measure.

  The tendency is to use a paper-and-pencil survey to measure just about everything that has to do with employee perceptions, but we have many different methods available to us: on-line surveys, focus groups, structured observation, logs and journals, and learning histories. The appropriateness of each of these methods depends on what kind of data are needed, the sources of that data, the circumstances for collecting the data, and how the data will be used. The method should make the thinking behind comments and behaviors explicit. Users of the evaluation want to *know-how* and *know-why*.

- Report data that are credible and useful to the customer.

  Line managers might accept the accuracy of employee interviews and focus groups, but senior executives might only
  listen to production and financial data. Know your audience
  so that you can collect measurement data and report
  findings that the key stakeholders will find convincing.

- Report findings so that the customer can hear them.

  This has to do with how the information is reported. You
  will want all of the various customers to understand your
  findings and be able to act on the implications. Keep it
  simple, relate it to the goals that are important to the particular audience, and recommend what should be done about
  the results. Do not just report numbers; tell the story about
  what the numbers mean to the organization.

- Measure the process as well as the outcome.

  Continuous improvement is achieved by regular assessment
  of where people are in the process of learning. Adjustments
  to the process can be made, especially as you find out more
  about employee needs and the organization becomes clearer
  about its goals.

- Provide just-in-time and just-enough information.

  Give employees the information they need, when and where
  they need it. Performance is maximized when people are not
  overwhelmed with new information, when they can relate
  new information to their work, and when they can apply the
  learning to a problem on the job immediately.

- Measure to improve the process, not to blame or punish.

  Our tendency is to feel threatened by anything that might
  reveal our personal incompetency. When we feel threatened,

we become less cooperative and less willing to improve performance. Do everything that you can to assure participants that the measures are not being used to make judgments about individuals. Follow through on this promise. Use the data only to make changes in the learning process and to plan for additional activities that will make a difference in performance.

• Evaluation is a powerful tool for organizational learning.

Used to evaluate the link between learning and enhanced capacity to achieve strategic goals, it can help you make your organization more successful. But this requires moving beyond assessing learners' immediate reactions to events and examining the entire process that facilitates individual, small-group, and whole-organization learning. The payoff comes when you use this information to improve the learning process and make sure the process has high impact on building the capacity of the organization.

CHAPTER XVI

Physical Environment

Is the physical environment of the workplace conducive to learning? Does the arrangement of work space and traffic flow facilitate communication among employees? Are the people who need to learn from each other coming into frequent contact?

Most workplace learning takes place in informal interactions. A casual hallway conversation among co-workers can lead to a discussion where people compare experiences with a new process. A chance meeting between managers can result in a new strategy for dealing with a supervision problem. A free-flowing, lunch-time discussion among work team members can lead to an innovation in how they do their work together.

Tom Peters wrote this in *Liberation Management*:

> Physical location issues are neither plain nor vanilla. In fact, space management may well be the most ignored—and most powerful—tool for inducing cultural change, speeding up innovation projects and enhancing the learning process in far flung organizations. While we rail ceaselessly about facilities issues such as office square-footage allotted to various ranks, we all but ignore the key strategic issue—the parameters of intermingling.

Most traditional work space is designed for maximum control and maintenance of hierarchy. Line and lower-level workers are on the inside, perhaps in cubicles or in an open space with production equipment, while senior managers and executives are in outer offices with one window on production and one window on the outside world. The higher your rank in the organization, the larger your office and the more sunlight. But if we ask the question, *What is the best design for organizational learning?* we would probably end up with a much different configuration and allocation of space.

On an individual level, the workplace should accommodate the wide range of differences in how people learn. Some people need a lot of quiet and solitude, while others need contact with people and intense activity.

On a small-group level, the workplace should accommodate a variety of different needs: face-to-face interaction, cross-functional interaction, a variety of meeting spaces, and space availability on short notice.

On a whole-organization level, the workplace structure should be a visible statement that reinforces the values espoused by the organization. If organizational learning is valued, the design and management of the facility should factor in access to the information, people, and technology that people need if they are to help achieve the business goals. Space and the way it is used will reflect who and what is valued by the organization.

You might not have the authority to build a new facility, but you can try to influence how interior spaces are designed and used. As with any task outside of your experience, you should seek help from an interior design consultant. Using the benchmarking method, you can see many good ideas implemented at

other companies. The major office-systems companies (s
as Steelcase, Haworth, or Herman Miller) will be eager
show you examples of how work space can be designed to
facilitate interaction and teamwork among employees.

Martha O'Mara suggests using decisions about the design of
the workplace to begin discussing the values and goals of your
organization. You can use the design problem to turn
employees' attention to the future and the organization's
strategic direction. You can ask, "If we have to live in this

---

SOME TIPS ON PHYSICAL ENVIRONMENT CONSIDERATIONS

- Make space considerations part of strategic planning.

- Use an open office plan, with work areas dedicated to
  teams whenever appropriate.

- Provide space for team members to meet formally
  whenever a meeting is necessary.

- Arrange people and offices so that informal, spontaneous
  contacts are frequent.

- Locate the technology so that employees have access
  when and where they need it.

- Give employees control over the comfort of their office
  environment (such as lighting, temperature, and
  furniture) whenever possible.

- Minimize noise and visual distractions for those
  employees whose responsibilities or learning styles
  demand it.

Based on research conducted by the American Society of
Interior Designers.

e for the next five years, what design would maximize our
rning and performance?"

The design and management of the workplace can contribute
to organizational learning.

CHAPTER XVII

Conclusion

I have painted the landscape of organizational learning for you. Your next step is to focus on the details: to learn more about those aspects of organizational learning that will prove most immediately helpful in your work.

Organizational learning is acquiring and applying knowledge at the individual, small-group, and whole-organization levels in order to build the capacity of the organization to achieve its strategic goals. Organizational learning is not simply a catalog of training programs, although training is a very important aspect of learning. Opportunities for learning and change are enormous in any complex organization, and they will become more obvious to you when you adopt a mental model of work as learning—when you accept the notion that you are in the business of organizational learning.

The keys to effective organizational learning? Reflection and feedback. These are what allow individuals and groups to learn from information. We are bombarded by information throughout the workday. Valuable learning occurs when we can take in this information, reflect on its meaning and value, use it in our work, and receive feedback from others regarding its effects.

...ob is to create conditions in which reflection and feedback ...me part of the normal work processes of your organization.

...hope this short book has provided you with concepts, approaches, and even a few tools *to help you help your organization learn*. You no doubt realize that some of the strategies I have described can be implemented on your own, whereas others will require assistance from experts. Remember: A good manager knows when (and where) to get help.

You have a critical role to play in organizational learning. As a manager, you can create the conditions that motivate, support, and enhance everyone's learning. Get started by filling out the self-audit below.

ORGANIZATIONAL LEARNING SELF-AUDIT		
Instructions: Answer these questions for your organization. Discuss your responses and their implications with co-workers.		
1. Are managers who support learning rewarded?	Yes	No
2. Is there reflection and feedback at the end of meetings?	Yes	No
3. Are learning opportunities provided as part of all meetings and gatherings of employees?	Yes	No
4. Can employees direct their own learning?	Yes	No
5. Does every job include some form of on-the-job training?	Yes	No

6. Do training events have planned preparation and follow-up components?   Yes   No

7. Are the principles of adult learning applied to training programs?   Yes   No

8. Are employee knowledge, skills, and attitudes linked to the strategic goals of the organization?   Yes   No

9. Do employees receive frequent formal and informal feedback on their job performance, and do they discuss what they need to learn in order to improve their performance?   Yes   No

10. Do employees have individualized learning plans?   Yes   No

11. Do managers have a mentor or coach who can help them implement their individualized learning plans?   Yes   No

12. Are managers clear about their coaching role with the people they supervise?   Yes   No

13. Is experimentation and risk-taking for the purpose of learning supported, and not punished?   Yes   No

14. Does the organization encourage and facilitate knowledge-management and best-practices transfer?   Yes   No

ORGANIZATIONAL LEARNING SELF-AUDIT (continued)

15. Do teams plan for group learning?   Yes   No

16. Are there opportunities for whole   Yes   No
    organization learning?

17. Are the physical space of the office   Yes   No
    and the service and production
    areas designed for learning and
    productivity?

PART FOUR

Resources

This section provides you with a list of books, articles, newsletters, Websites, and professional organizations that can help you acquire a deeper understanding of organizational learning. The resources are separated into four categories: (1) general organizational learning; (2) individual learning; (3) small-group learning; and (4) whole-organization learning.

al Organizational Learning: References

ris, Chris. *Overcoming Organizational Defenses*. Allyn and Bacon, 1990.

rgyris, Chris, and Donald Schon. *Theory in Practice*. San Francisco: Jossey-Bass, 1974.

Ashkenas, Ron, Dave Ulrich, Todd Jick, and Steve Kerr. *The Boundaryless Organization: Breaking the Chains of Organizational Structure*. San Francisco: Jossey-Bass, 1995.

Bass, Bernard. *Leadership and Performance Beyond Expectations*. New York: The Free Press, 1985.

Brinkerhoff, Robert O., and S.J. Gill. *The Learning Alliance: Systems Thinking in Human Resource Development*. San Francisco: Jossey-Bass, 1994.

Frydman, B., I. Wilson, and J. Wyer. *Organizational Learning: An Explorer's Guide*. San Francisco: Butterworth-Heinemann, 2000.

Future-at-Work: http://www.Future-At-Work.org

Garvin, David A. Building a Learning Organization. *Harvard Business Review*, July-August 1993, pp. 78–79.

Gill, Stephen J. Shifting Gears for High Performance. *Training and Development*, May 1995, pp. 25–31.

Goleman, Daniel. What Makes a Leader? *Harvard Business Review*, November–December 1998, pp. 93–102.

Haines, Stephen G. *The Manager's Pocket Guide to Systems Thinking and Learning*. Amherst, MA: HRD Press, 1998.

Institute for Research on Learning: www.irl.org

Kim, Daniel H. *Healthcare Forum Journal*. July/August 1993.

Leverage. Published by Pegasus Communications: www. pegasuscom.com

Marquardt, Michael J. *Building the Learning Organization*. New York: McGraw Hill, 1996.

Organizational Development Network: www.odnet.org

Pegasus Communications, Inc.: www.pegasuscom.com

Reflections: The SoL Journal on Knowledge, Learning, (Change. MIT Press.

Rubin, Harriet. The New Merchants of Light. *Leader to Leader*, Fall 1998, pp. 34–40.

Schein, Edgar H. Can Learning Cultures Evolve? *The Systems Thinker*, Vol. 7, No. 6, August 1996, pp. 1–5.

Senge, Peter. M. The Leader's New Work: Building Learning Organizations. *Sloan Management Review*, Vol. 32, No. 1, Fall 1990, pp. 7–22.

Senge, Peter. *The Fifth Discipline: The Art and Practice of the Learning Organization.* New York: Doubleday/Currency, 1990.

Senge, Peter, A. Kleiner, C. Roberts, R.B. Ross, and B.J. Smith. *The Fifth Discipline Fieldbook.* New York: Doubleday/ Currency, 1994. www.fieldbook.com/ rlearning.html

Senge, Peter, A. Kleiner, C. Roberts, R. Ross, G. Roth, and B. Smith. *The Dance of Change.* New York: Doubleday/ Currency, 1999.

Society for Organizational Learning: www.sol-ne.org

The Systems Thinker. Newsletter published by Pegasus Communications: www.pegasus.com

Thompson, John W. The Renaissance of Learning in Business. In *Learning Organizations: Developing Cultures for Tomorrow's Workplace.* Portland, OR: Productivity Press, 1995.

Tobin, Daniel R. *Knowledge-Enabled Organization.* New York: AMACOM, 1998.

Watkins, Karen E., and V.J. Marsick. In *Action: Creating the Learning Organization.* ASTD Press.

ual Learning: References

.ican Productivity and Quality Center

.erican Society for Training and Development: www.astd.org

Argyris, Chris. Good Communication that Blocks Learning. *Harvard Business Review*, July–August 1994.

Argyris, Chris. Teaching Smart People How to Learn. *Harvard Business Review*, May–June 1991, pp. 5–15.

Carnevale, A. P., and L.J. Gainer. *The Learning Enterprise.* Alexandria, VA: American Society for Training and Development and U.S. Department of Labor, 1989.

Cory, Diane, and R. Bradley. Partnership Coaching. *The Systems Thinker*, Vol. 9, No. 4, May 1998, pp. 1–5.

Daudelin, Marilyn W., and D.T. Hall. Using Reflection to Leverage Learning. *Training and Development*, December 1997, pp. 13–14.

Fisher, Sharon G. *The Manager's Pocket Guide to Performance Management.* Amherst, MA: HRD Press, 1997.

Flaherty, James. *Coaching: Evoking Excellence in Others.* Boston: Butterworth-Heinemann, 1999.

Gallway, T. *The Inner Game of Work: Building Capacity in the Workplace.*

Gery, Gloria J. *Electronic Performance Support Systems.* Boston: Weingarten Publications, 1991.

Gilley, Jerry W., N. W. Boughton, and A. Maycunich. *The Performance Challenge.* Reading, MA: Perseus Books, 1999.

Hiam, Alexander. *The Manager's Pocket Guide to Creativity.* Amherst, MA: HRD Press, 1998.

International Society for Performance Improvement

Jacobs, R.L., and M.J. Jones. *Structured On-the-Job Training.* San Francisco: Berrett-Kohler, 1995.

Kim, Daniel H. The Link between Individual and ~~Organi~~-zational Learning. *Sloan Management Review*, Fall Vol. 35, No. 1, pp. 37–50.

Library of Congress Internet Resource: www.loc.go~ global/internet/training.html

Richey, Rita. *The Theoretical and Conceptual Bases of Instructional Design*. New York: Nichols Publishing, 1986.

Shea, Gordon F. *Mentoring*. Menlo Park, CA: Crisp Publications, 1992.

Stamps, David. Enterprise Training: This Changes Everything. *TRAINING*, January 1999, pp. 41–48.

The Training Café (online Web technology instruction): http://www.trainingcafe.com

TRAINING Magazine: www.trainingsupersite.com

Training Zone (news, tools, discussion): http://www.trainingzone.co.uk/index.html

Vaill, Peter. *Learning as a Way of Being: Strategies for Survival in a World of Permanent White Water*. San Francisco: Jossey-Bass, 1996.

Web-Based Training Information Center: filename.com/wbt/index.html

Small-Group Learning: References

Bennett, Sherrin, and Juanita Brown. Mindshift: Strategic Dialogue for Breakthrough Thinking. In *Learning Organizations: Developing Cultures for Tomorrow's Workplace*, S. Chawla and J. Renesch, eds. Portland, OR: Productivity Press, 1995, pp. 167–183.

Brown, Juanita, and David Isaacs. Conversation as a Core Business Process. *The Systems Thinker*, Vol. 7, No. 10, Dec. 1996/Jan. 1997.

avid. *On Dialogue*. David Bohm Seminars, 1990.

..., A., D. Sibbet, and R. Forrester. The Team Performance Model. In *Team Building: Blueprints for Productivity and Satisfaction*. NTL Institute and University Associates, 1994.

Foy, Nancy. Action Learning Comes to Industry. *Harvard Business Review*, September/October 1977, pp. 158–159.

Garvin, David A. Asking Questions Is the Skill Needed for "Discussion Teaching." *Chronicle of Higher Education*, July 25, 1984, p. 20.

Gerzon, Mark. Mediators Foundation, 3833 N. 57th Street, Boulder, CO 80301 and The Public Conversations Project, National Study Circles Resources, The Common Enterprise (handout).

Katzenbach, J.R., and D.K. Smith. *The Wisdom of Teams: Creating the High-Performance Organization*. Harvard Business School Press, 1993.

Killion, J., and C. Harrison. The Practice of Reflection: An Essential Learning Process. *The Developer*, December 1991/January 1992, National Staff Development Council.

Kleiner, Art, and George Roth. How to Make Experience Your Company's Best Teacher. *Harvard Business Review*, September–October 1997, pp. 172–177.

Learning History Research Project, The: http://www.ccs.mit.edu./LH?

Losada, Marcial. The Complex Dynamics of High Performance Teams. *Mathematical and Computer Modelling*, Vol. 30 (9–19), 1999, pp. 179–192.

Russ-Eft, Darlene, Hallie Preskill, and Catherine Sleezer.

Human Resource Development Review. Thous.
Oaks, CA: Sage Publications, 1997.

Yankelovich, Daniel. *The Magic of Dialogue: Transforming Conflict into Cooperation*. New York: Simon and Schuster, 1999.

Whole-Organization Learning: References

Axelrod, E.M., and R.H. Axelrod. The Conference Model (R). In *The Change Handbook*, P. Holman and J. Devane, eds. San Francisco: Berrett-Koehler, 1999, pp. 263–278.

Buchanan, Leigh. The Smartest Little Company in America. *Inc.*, January 1999, pp. 43–54.

Chawla, Sarita, and John Renesch, eds. *Learning Organizations: Developing Cultures for Tomorrow's Workplace*. Portland, OR: Productivity Press, 1995.

de Geus, Arie. Planning as Learning. *Harvard Business Review*, March/April 1988.

de Geus, Arie. *The Living Company*. Boston: Harvard Business School Press, 1997.

DiBella, Anthony. *How Organizations Learn: An Integrated Strategy for Building Learning Capability*. Jossey-Bass, 1998.

Dilworth, Robert. The DNA of the Learning Organization. In *Learning Organizations: Developing Cultures for Tomorrow's Workplace*. Portland, OR: Productivity Press, 1995, pp. 243–255.

Dodd, Pamela. *Pushing the Boundaries: Learning Organization Lessons from the Field*. Ann Arbor: Kennedy Press, Inc., 1998.

Forrester, Jay W. Counterintuitive Behavior of Social Systems. *Theory and Decision*, 2, 1971, pp. 109–140.

⌐, Sue Annis. *The Thin Book of Appreciative Inquiry.* ⌐no, TX: The Thin Book Publishing Company, 1998.

⌐t, Marc. The Limits of Benchmarking. *Training*, February 1993, pp. 36–41.

⌐lman, Peggy, and Tom Devane, eds. *The Change Handbook.* Berrett-Koehler, 1999.

Kauffman, Draper L., Jr. *Systems 1: An Introduction to Systems Thinking.* Minneapolis: S.A. Carlton, 1980.

Kellogg Leadership Studies Project

Kim, Daniel H. *Systems Thinking Tools: A User's Reference Guide.* Cambridge, MA, 1995.

Kiser, Kim. Working on World Time. *Training*, March 1999, pp. 29–34.

Lippitt, Lawrence L. *Preferred Futuring.* San Francisco: Berrett-Koehler Publishers, Inc., 1998.

Meinholf, D., J. Child, and Y. Nonaka. *The Handbook of Organizational Learning.* Oxford: Oxford University Press, 1998.

Noer, Peter M. *Breaking Free: A Prescription for Personal and Organizational Change.* San Francisco: Jossey-Bass.

Nonaka, Ikujiro. The Knowledge-Creating Company. *Harvard Business Review*, November-December 1991, pp. 96–104.

O'Dell, Carla, and C. Jackson Grayson. *If Only We Knew What We Know.* New York: The Free Press, 1998.

O'Mara, Martha A. *Strategy and Place.* New York: The Free Press, 1999.

Owen, Harrison. *Open Space Technology: A User's Guide. 2nd ed.* San Francisco: Barrett-Koehler, 1997.

Peters, Tom. *Liberation Management.* New York: Fawcett, 1992.

Preskill, Hallie, and Rosalie T. Torres. *Evaluative Inquiry for Learning in Organizations.* Thousand Oaks, CA: Sage Publications, 1999.

Rummler, Geary A., and Alan P. Brache. *Improving Perf... How To Manage the White Space on the Organizatio...* San Francisco: Jossey-Bass, 1990.

Schein, Edgar H. How Can Organizations Learn Faster: Challenge of Entering the Green Room. *Sloan Manageme... Review*, Vol. 34(2), Winter 1993.

Schein, Edgar H. *Organizational Culture and Leadership.* San Francisco: Jossey-Bass, 1985.

Schein, Edgar H. Organizational Learning: What Is New? http://www.learning.mit.edu/res/wp/10012.html

Stamps, David. Learning Ecologies. *Training*, January 1998, pp. 32–38.

Van Buren, Mark E. A Yardstick for Knowledge Management. *Training and Development*, May 1999, pp. 71–78.

Weisbord, Marvin R. *Productive Workplaces: Organizing and Managing for Dignity, Meaning, and Community.* San Francisco: Jossey-Bass, 1987.

Weisbord, Marvin R., and Sandra Janoff. *Future Search: An Action Guide to Finding Common Ground in Organizations and Communities.* San Francisco: Barrett-Koehler, 1995.

Wheatley, Margaret J. Leading through the Unknowns of Y2K. *The Systems Thinker*, Dec. 1998/Jan. 1999, pp. 1–5.

Whole Systems Associates' World Café site: www.theworld-cafe.com

Wilson, Iva M. *Organizational Change at Philips Display Components: Reflections on a Learning Journey.* Innovations in Management Series. Waltham, MA: Pegasus Communications, 1999.

Zemke, Ron. Don't Fix That Company. *Training Magazine*, June 1999, pp. 26–33.

INDEX

About the Author

Stephen J. Gill, Ph.D., is an independent consultant with over 20 years of experience in employee training and performance improvement. He works with a wide variety of for-profit, not-for-profit, and government organizations analyzing their learning needs and evaluating the effectiveness of their training and development programs. He helps individuals, teams, and organizations learn from their experiences and use information to achieve their strategic goals. He has published nearly 40 articles, book chapters, and books as well as handbooks and manuals related to professional learning and development. He earned his Ph.D. in counseling psychology from Northwestern University and was on the faculty of The University of Michigan School of Education before going into consulting 10 years ago. He is co-author of *The Learning Alliance: Systems Thinking in Human Resource Development,* published by Jossey-Bass in 1994.